THE GLOBAL BELIEVER

Ingo Swann's surrealistic painting, *Salt Flats Vision,* evokes the feelings of emergence found in Joseph Donders's *The Global Believer.* The cosmic egg, suspended as a still point, invites one to make the journey of discovery into the mystery of the self and the wonders of a new creation.

Foreword by Rev. Richard Rohr, ofm

THE GLOBAL BELIEVER

Toward A New
Imitation
of
Christ

Joseph G. Donders

TWENTY-THIRD PUBLICATIONS
Mystic, Connecticut

Twenty-Third Publications
P.O. Box 180
Mystic, CT 06355
(203) 536-2611

ISBN 0-89622-294-2
Library of Congress Catalog Card Number 86-50238

Cover by George Herrick
Edited and designed by John G. van Bemmel

Cover Art: *Salt Flats Vision* by Ingo Swann. The 45″
× 50″ canvas is on display in the National Air and
Space Museum, Smithsonian Institution, Washington,
D.C.

FOREWORD

*I*t has wisely been said that "the problem with our society and politics is its sinful presumption that man is born to be happy, when he clearly has to die. A truthful politics is one that teaches us to die for the right thing, and only the church can be trusted with that task...and that task is to be faithful to the story of God that makes intelligible the divided nature of the world" (Stanley Hauerwas).

I believe Joseph Donders is not only being "faithful to the story of God" in these pages, but is also calling the church to its own task and conversion, to dying for the right things, and to the still surprising discovery of an excess of happiness—besides! This kind of book is preparing believers for the unfolding age, for the Christ who is still coming, for the Kingdom that we are never ready for and do not really want. My only disappointment is that some Christians might not read it. Or worse, others might read it and not realize how revolutionary it is—in comparison to much of our lived Christian history.

We have not yet made "intelligible the divided nature of the world." In fact, we live in an age and country that seem to profoundly aggravate that division, being afraid of "the other," and projecting their own darkness onto other races, ideologies, and world views. We ask if there is ever going to be any way out of such blindness and arrogance? *The Global Believer* shows us a way that is both very traditional and utterly new. It must be Gospel.

Too long the Gospel has been wrapped in European prejudices and unwittingly carried Western assumptions. As we made "disciples of all nations" it was too often disciple-ship to English education, French tastes, or American pragmatism. Jesus had to squeeze in on the side, trying desperately to shed his colonial dress in favor of a reconcil-ing, universal message. Frankly, it is hard for us all to ad-mit that Jesus is calling his people beyond self-interest, beyond the national security state, beyond the nuclear fami-ly. We have used Jesus for our own purposes for so long that we are not sure we want to return to him his sovereign-ty, his lordship over church and history. Gratefully, however, in our time challenging and complementing voices come from every continent shouting, "Come, Lord Jesus. Come, Cosmic Christ!"

The "new spiritual style" that this book calls for is real-ly a return to a wholistic and very honest faith, a faith that refuses to hide behind religious jargon, a faith that begins by trusting, pondering, and sharing our simple and univer-sal human experiences. No elitism here. This is the not-for-professionals mysticism that John's Gospel takes for granted among believers. Here the ego is centered and in size: neither too large as in the West, nor incapable of mutuality as in the East. In such faith and prayer, "we experience be-ing the center of the universe. But we know, and feel, that the universe does not depend on us." We don't just need one another; we also need one another's vantage point. As the African student says, "We are made up in two's."

This book might be difficult for the entrenched. And the author is expert in revealing the many kinds of trenches we sit in. We can hole up in the scholastic perspective, just as easily as we can hide in contemporary personalism, or shout angrily from a place of liberated righteousness. We can save the whales while losing our own soul. But most of us have lived through the post-Vatican II era with enough savvy to now recognize that the liberal agenda is fraught with in-dividualism and self-interest, just as much as the traditional agenda was. It's only the language that has changed, albeit a bit more psychological and sophisticated now.

Joe Donders rightly calls us all to our inner still point, to an inner and outer journey—simultaneously but definitively—and from there, as Jesus to Jerusalem, back to the Center. He is wise to caution the modern reader against timidity in either journey. Our very "outerness" makes true contemplation very difficult. We do not easily move to the level of Being and Mystery, unless there is some payback on the consumer plane. Neither are we anxious to move beyond the level of psyche, feeling, and attitude, toward responsible action and solidarity with human suffering. In these areas we must own our biases and temperaments. All of us must move or be moved from "here" to "there." That is the notorious work of conversion. After fifteen years as a pastor of a lay community and retreat master, I have no illusions about the urgency and the difficulty of this task.

I only met Fr. Joseph Donders once. I was on a preaching tour in Africa when I was asked to address the students after the Saturday night Eucharist at the University of Nairobi. Fortunately, Fr. Donders was the celebrant and homilist, and I had the grand opportunity to see him in action in his own congregation. He had a message. He knew it. He knew how to deliver it, with conviction and just enough entertaining drama to engage them. They listened with wrapt attention. And finally *they* knew it. The message and the messenger had done their job: the Gospel was again proclaimed, "cutting like any double-edged sword but more finely, slipping through the place where the soul is divided from the spirit, or joints from the marrow, judging our secret emotions and thoughts" (Hebrews 4:12). This book will do the same.

And you are forewarned. Perhaps I can use the intended compliment that was recently given to me after a preached retreat of my own: "He assiduously avoids diverting you with a single merely 'pious' thought!"

Richard Rohr, O.F.M.
Cincinnati, Ohio

CONTENTS

INTRODUCTION

This book on spirituality tries to discover from a spiritual point of view what is living in us. That sounds forbidding, but it isn't.

You might object: "Don't I know best what is happening to me? I don't really need a book on my spirituality." In a way, you don't; it's your experience that is under study. But in a way, you do.

As far as our spiritual experiences are concerned, we are like artists who work with models and symbols to express what is in them. Though authors write, painters paint, and poets make poems, they don't always understand what it is they create, or what is coming over them as they create. They sometimes remark, "I don't know where it all comes from!" That awareness is more often revealed by their critics who analyze their work. It is the literary critics who sometimes make the authors understand what they wrote and why.[1]

This book is about what is spiritually alive in us; it is about our contemporary belief and a variety of attitudes and world visions that compound our belief. These attitudes and experiences are changing very rapidly, but not chaotically. We have to find our way among them in order to live our lives in the light of them.

This book is written within the Western tradition of those who refer, or used to refer, to the Bible to make sense of their lives. Fewer and fewer people seem to do that these days. They often look elsewhere for further or different inspiration, but don't stop searching for answers to their fundamental questions of life.

Their search has intensified as they look around in the universe and often consider themselves the center of it all.

1

Isn't that a fundamental experience of the modern Western personality?[2]

Some are the center of the universe in a private way. They shrink away from life where they have to face the frightening potential of nuclear annihilation, economic collapse, social unrest, and ecological disaster. In a kind of self-defense, they make minimal contact with themselves, though they might have worked out a very clear operational plan in view of their careers. They have collapsed upon themselves, walking with two earphones on their heads, apparently isolated from their neighbors. Yet, even the earphones indicate less individualism than they would like to admit, being plugged in to others, as they are; a window is kept open to the wide electronic world, listening to music, an international discussion, the results of the stock exchange, a novel, or even a church service.

Others see themselves the center of the universe in a much more public way. They find more and more pleasure in discovering the world in themselves. They feel wrapped within mystery and myth every moment of their lives. They are global in their interests, in their business, and in their beliefs.

We live in a world where religious beliefs and moral values often seem to have disappeared.

Missionaries and other travelers in foreign cultures were often so unaccustomed to, and surprised by, the new lifestyles they found that they thought there were no values at all in those cultures. The religiousness and morality they found were sometimes so different from theirs that they usually thought them to be inauthentic or outright evil. At the moment, much of the religious leadership, and the majority of the faithful believers, seem to be in the same position regarding the world around them. They don't seem to find anything of value. What the world offers seems empty to them. Vanity of vanity, as *The Imitation of Christ*, quoting Sirach, noted so long ago. As a consequence, what they themselves say to the world sounds empty and useless to their hearers.

A new spiritual style is called for. We can't expect people to be naturally spiritual, as religious leaders often do, and to conclude at the same time that "we don't find any spirituality in our world today." It must be there. Where is it? How do we find it? How can it bring us together? These are serious questions. According to Iris Murdoch, it is the essential and only question of our age:

> I have also been led at last to a clear understanding of my true vocation. I, and others (how many are we, I wonder), are *chosen* to strive for continuance of religion on this planet. Nothing else but *true religion* can save mankind from a lightless and irredeemable materialism, from a technocratic nightmare where determinism *becomes true* for all except an *unimaginable depraved* few, who are themselves the mystified slaves of a conspiracy of machines. The challenge has gone forth and in the deep catacombs the spirit has stirred to a new life. But can we be in time, can religion survive and not, with us, utterly perish?[3]

1

YOU
AS CENTER
OF THE UNIVERSE

I am the center of the universe. So are you. As far as I am concerned, the whole of the universe is there for me, not only the reality I vaguely call nature, but all artistic, scientific, and technological developments as well. Bertrand Russell told the story of a small boy he once saw at a fountain in the middle of the town square. The boy would look for a moment at the fountain, then look away from it, and then, as quickly as he could, look back at the fountain. Intrigued by this strange behavior, the great philosopher asked the boy what he was doing. He answered, "I am trying to see if the fountain remains there, even while I'm not looking!" The fountain must have been standing in for the whole of the boy's lifetime. He was trying to find out whether it was there only for him.

Most of the time we live in our universe in the middle of a multitude of other persons and things. We are limited by time and space; we experience the resistance of the things and people around us. We feel hampered, stereotyped, frustrated, closed in, helpless, and often even hopeless. It is not always like that. We have other moments; we often call them our

4

peak experiences. They are moments of ecstasy and self-awareness when all limitations and barriers fall away and we feel one with the universe around and within us.

A Leaping Ecstasy

Descriptions of that state have often been recorded in modern literature. Here's a description by Irish novelist Forest Reid:

> It was as if I had never realized how lovely the world was. I lay down on my back in the warm, dry moss and listened to the skylark singing as it mounted up from the field near the sea into the dark clear sky. No other music ever gave me the same pleasure as that passionate, joyous singing. It was a kind of leaping, exultant ecstasy, a bright flame-like sound, rejoicing in itself. And then a curious experience befell me. It was as if everything that seemed to be external and around me were suddenly within me. It was within me that the trees waved their green branches, it was within me that the skylark was singing, it was within me that the hot sun shone, and that the shade was cool. A cloud rose in the sky, and passed in a light shower that pattered on the leaves, and I felt its freshness dropping into my soul, and I felt in all my being the delicious fragrance of the earth and the grass and the plants and the rich brown soil. I could have sobbed with joy.[1]

This type of experience can be very different. Some people have it when they swim in the cool water of a lake on a warm summer evening. They undress and swim naked in the water, and suddenly it is as if the water, and the trees, and the shore, and the breeze, and the sky, and they themselves all flowed together: they feel one with all and everything. A great peace comes over them and they know that nothing can happen to them, that all is good and safe.

The North American philosopher William James gives this description of such a happening:

> I was alone upon the seashore as all these thoughts flowed over me, liberating and reconciling; and now again, as once

before in distant days in the Alps of Dauphine, I was impelled to kneel down, this time for the illimitable ocean, symbol of the Infinite. I felt that I prayed as I never had prayed before, and knew now what prayer really is: to return from the solitude of individuation into the consciousness of unity with all that is, to kneel down as one that passes away, and to rise up as one imperishable. Earth, heaven, and sea resounded as in one vast world-encircling harmony. It was as if the chorus of all the great who had ever loved were about me. I felt myself one with them, and it appeared as if I heard the greeting: "Thou too belongest to the company of those who have overcome."[2]

James not only felt one with nature, but also with humanity, though he restricted himself only to the great people.

This feeling of unity happens not only when we are contemplating nature; it can take place in very different ways. Many have it when confronted with the beginning of life and the end of it; some have it when they join in singing a patriotic song or religious hymn; others when they listen to music, e.g., the concluding chorus of the Ninth Symphony by Beethoven; when they read a book, when they admire a painting or a sculpture, when they pray or embrace a loved one. It is always a process of self-discovery.

Unfolding Within Ourselves

All these experiences can open us up and lead to new breakthroughs, to further inner expression and unfolding. Every artist, every mystic had this intuition. Author Herman Melville once told Hawthorne: "Until I was twenty-five I had no development at all. From my twenty-fifth year I date my life. Three weeks have scarcely passed, at any time between then and now, that I have not unfolded within myself."[3]

In the case of the French author, Marcel Proust, even the smallest incident was able to do that. It might be the reason for the lasting, modern interest for his long-winded books. In one of them he tells how one afternoon, while being depressed and very bored, his mother offered him a cup of tea with some cookies. Proust dipped a cooky (romantically called *Petite Madeleine*) into his tea.

> But at the very moment when the mouthful mixed with the crumbs of the cake touched my palate, I shuddered as I took note of the strange things that were going on inside me. An exquisite pleasure had invaded me, isolated, with no idea of what its cause might be. Immediately it had made the vicissitudes of life indifferent, its disasters inoffensive, its brevity illusory, in much the same way as love operates, filling me with a precious essence; or rather this essence was not *in* me, it *was* me. I had ceased to feel mediocre, contingent, or mortal. Whence should this strong joy have come to me? I felt that it was connected with the taste of the tea and the cake, but that it transcended it infinitely and could not be of the same nature. Whence did it come? What did it mean? How to lay hold of it?[4]

Proust compares the feeling he experienced with love: "the same way as love operates." It is in love, while embracing each other, that lovers experience and express their belonging to the whole of the universe and to each other in the most obvious way.

Many might still have the feeling described by Thomas à Kempis in *The Imitation of Christ*, quoting Seneca: "As often as I have been among men, I have returned home a lesser man."[5] A more comtemporary reaction to such a meeting after a workshop was:

> They were such nice days with such fine people, and about a subject that really touched my "existence." Driving home, such a strong feeling of happiness hit me that I burst out in tears. It had nothing to do with my love for one person, or so. It was more a deeply felt feeling of being one with God, and everyone, and everything.[6]

This feeling of being interconnected and one, of being the center of it all, is not only something in the spiritual or psychological field. It also has its physical, technical, and bodily aspects.

Mother Earth Dressed in White and Blue

When reading the latest news in a paper, watching it on television, or listening to it on a far-off shortwave radio, we always wonder how the news will affect us. It seems to be the only reason we are interested. The war in the Middle East might mean that I won't be able to buy the gas I need. A strike in Japan might increase my chances of a promotion here at home. A conflict in South America might jeopardize the holiday trip I intended to make to Rio de Janeiro. A change of leadership in Russia might mean that I am going to be drafted for military service.

The same is true of the more private news that affects family, our relationships, or our work environment. Anything that happens is seen from my point of view, I being the center. There does not seem to be anything that happens in our contemporary world that does not have its effects on me and on all of us. These effects are not limited only to what we ourselves undergo, but also influence others because of the impact my decisions have on them.

We are "hanging together" in a kind of web—each one being a gossamer strand—in all we decide to do or not do. We all form one body.

The most spectacular development in our day is in the field of communications. When speaking about "progress" today, we almost always speak about that aspect of our life. Means of communication are means of being interconnected. Many authors and speakers have observed that our world is growing together, but hardly anyone draws the right conclusions. We remain stuck in metaphors; we get lost in mere talk. Isn't humanity really growing together? Don't our means of communication—extending the functions of our personal bodies and senses — really bridge the distances that still exist between individuals and groups. Aren't we together in such a way that we realistically form one body? It is no longer only poetry or a figure of speech that we call our roads arteries. When there was a blackout in the eastern United States in 1965, it was not without significance that reporters spoke about it in terms of high blood pressure. The people struck by the power failure lost their connections with others, since they were plugged into the same energy system. Connections fell apart, literally. People were suddenly divided into rather individuated cells. Immediately an old lifestyle came back, living without electrical conveniences. The fact that people still remembered and mastered that old lifestyle was their salvation.

It is against a person's human rights to pierce his or her eardrums, or to remove someone's hearing aid. Doesn't one infringe on the same rights by denying someone access to telephone, radio, television, and other ways of communication since such means of communication is necessary in our world for participation in life and culture? Telephone, telex, computer networks connect all of us. Life has become something communal. We are, we have, we form one body. Although a scientific mystic like Pierre Teilhard de Chardin could speak only in the vaguest terms about this concept, it has become a concrete reality. Russian author Yevgeny Yevtushenko writes:

> Tsiolkovsky thought: The only thing that could end war forever is changing the human psyche. Those who fly up above earth and see her in all her beauty and fragility will undergo a psychological change. At first only individuals, but then hundreds, then millions. It will be a different civilization, a different humanity. They will reevaluate the earth's beauty, the taste of each of her berries.[7]

These astronauts see our Mother Earth, from whom we all are born, as a lady dressed in white and blue! Isn't it amazing to hear them echo those intuitions from the past? We have to reorganize our old thinking patterns from this astronautical point of view.

Take our aid to the so-called Third World. That aid is neither mere charity nor just a matter of justice. It is more. If my hands attend to my hurting eyes, I don't speak about charity or justice. Those categories don't even come into my mind in such a case. It is a normal, instinctive reaction of self-preservation. If we take our common human bodyliness seriously, we have to act in the same way with others.

It is remarkable how new-testamentic we are when we act in this way. The one body and the one spirit are gospel themes. They are also themes in so many other mystic inspirations and artistic intuitions.

A Fluid Divinity in All

In October 1984, Zairean Cardinal Malula gave a talk at a conference in Yaounde, the capital of Cameroon, in West Africa. The lecture was on the Western type of Christian marriage. That type of marriage was, according to the Cardinal, unacceptable to Africans, because, he said, we Africans see ourselves in a different way than Western people do. "In the West they consider themselves atoms."

This is an interesting remark. Malula compared the Western search for self-understanding with the models Western science was accustomed to use to understand the world. He made a mistake thinking that we in the West still consider the world as composed of mere atoms, or particles. His point was that we explain *ourselves* in the way we explain the world around us from a scientific point of view.

Did we come to think in terms of atoms — indivisible in themselves and divided from all others — when we tried to explain the universe, because we ourselves were already individualized? Or did we become individualized because we were thinking about reality as composed of atoms? Whatever the answer, there is a relation between the two.

At the moment, we no longer consider the atomistic model as a adequate description of the physical world. By now we know that this model has to be complemented by other models. We should think not only of atoms, but of waves, quants, quarks, and of electronic fields. So even when we think in terms of atoms, we complement that model in ways that connect those atoms and put them in relational fields.

It is the same for ourselves. Even if we think in terms of pure individualism, we consider our individuality as part of a relational field, and even containing in itself the whole of the universe. The experience of being the center of the universe was illustrated scientifically in a way at the discovery of the hologram. Doesn't each fragment of a hologram contain the whole of it? And can't each fragment be used to reconstitute the totality of it? This scientific model helps us to understand our human situation. Or did we discover the hologram, because we knew that each of us contains the whole of the universe?[8]

It is interesting to note that in the third Roman Catholic Episcopal Conference in 1884, the American bishops stressed the need to emphasize the devotion to the person of Jesus Christ as a model relating to the "American quest for individual greatness." That was the atomistic model of that time.

At the same conference, however, they also spoke about God as a "fluid divinity in all." That was the correction of a mere atomistic model: the atom and the wave. How did they know?

Good Shepherd of Our Universe

We were taught not to make ourselves the center of the universe. Of course, we are the center of it. We cannot help it; it is how we were made and how we experience ourselves. And since our universe is the only one we know, experience, and feel, we are, indeed, the center of *the* universe. But precisely at the moment we do not live this truth, we become what educators did not want us to be or become: self-centered.

Being the way we are, we have to be faithful to the universe we are the center of. We have to be, in the words of Martin Heidegger, good shepherds, good stewards to all and everything. This attitude seems to be the only truthful approach to contemporary reality. But we should not use the word "contemporary." The experience is not new. It has affected many before us: Jesus, Muhammed, Francis of Assisi, Buddha, Baha-u-lla, Gandhi, the pygmies in the Zairean rain forest, and so many others in all kinds of cultures definitely had this intuition.

Jesus is a very good example. When he was asked to define himself, he always did so in reference to the rest of humanity, describing himself as a part of a tree, the tree of life. He related to flowers, plants, birds, the sun, and the moon. He insisted that he was a member of the whole human family:

> Who are my mother and my brothers? And looking at those sitting in a circle around him, he said: Here are my mother and my brothers. Anyone who does the will of God, that person is my brother and sister and mother.[9]

Starting to understand and to live this truth seems at this point of our common history vital for the survival of humanity. We must live according to the truth about ourselves.

One of the greatest difficulties in our time is that we know we should be growing in community, but we still want to remain individuals. It is the struggle in the East and West. It is the cause of the difficulties between those two worlds. There will be a more or less desperate renaissance of the individual on the threshold of our communalization, because one defends most passionately what one is on the point of losing. Often a certain degree of obstinacy indicates that the defenders know that the old heritage has been lost already. A business often flourished just before its liquidation, and that because the end was in sight. The facade and the offices were renewed because of that threatening end. The terminal patient frequently has a remission just before dying.

With that understanding we can explain much that happened in the past and is happening around us. Even the difficulties to come in the future can be foreseen from this point of view.

The Inner and the Outer

We are often moved by the suffering of others. The possibility of our sympathy and compassion is another indication that we are the center of the universe. Why should I feel with others if I am not connected with them in one way or another?

Compassion means to let your heart speak. It tells us that not only our fellow human beings, but the animals and the plants, too, are of the same flesh and blood as we are.

There are plenty of considerations on the economic, social, and the further alienating conditions of the poor. We see others die of starvation on our television screens while we are drinking the coffee that they have picked.

We can easily have access to all the data of others suffering, but this knowledge does not seem to work if it does not really move us. It moves us only insofar as it touches something in us called compassion.

The people of the gospel story who left the beaten merchant along the roadside were possibly very pious, very religious, well informed, and perhaps even well to do. They passed by because they were without compassion. Their hearts were not moved.

Almost two centuries ago, Isabelle de Charriere, Belle de Zuylen, wrote in one of her letters:

> The white European does not include the black African in his idea of human society; to us a Turk slave does not belong to it, no more than the inhabitant of the American forests.

> What is that human society then? A word that we respect as it conveys to us the confused idea of an *arrangement* by which our habits remain unchanged, our possessions uninvaded, our ideas and prejudices sheltered from the trouble of re-examination. The numbers of sufferers so large, that of enjoyers so small.

That exclusion of the others from the world of the powerful is the reason for the powerlessness of the poor. It is the reason for the lack of compassion among the "enjoyers" and for the poverty and misery of the "sufferers." If we cut ourselves off from the others, or if we are cut off from them because of a depression, we are in hell. In his book *Wisdom, Madness and Folly: The Philosophy of a Lunatic*, John Custance describes hell:

> There I was shut in my own private universe as it were, with no contact with real people at all. . . . In the Kingdom of hell which depression reveals, the ego is not merely cut off; it is also increasingly restricted, until is seems to become

an almost infinitesimal point of abject misery, disgust, pain, and fear.[10]

We not only are the center of the universe, we *should* be the center. We should live the truth about ourselves. To speak in the words attributed to Jesus in the apocryphal Gospel of Thomas: "If you bring forth what is within you, what you bring forth will save you. If you do not bring forth what is within you, what you do not bring forth will kill you.[11]

There are two directions you can take in your life, an outward journey and an inward. You can take the inner route and the outer. You should take both, to discover yourself and the universe.

2

DEPENDING ON "THE ONE INVOKED"

You agree with what you read in this book or you don't. If you like the book it's because you recognize your ideas in it. They might make you feel good; they might not. If they do, they might make you grow. But this does not mean that you wrote the book. Take a poem you like very much. It brings something out in you that you had never even supposed to be there. You really feel like the poet. There is a striking harmony between your feelings and the sentiments expressed. But you did not write the poem!

It is the same regarding the experiences we have just described. We feel one with nature; we feel intimately related to the whole of humanity. Space and time, the present, the past, and the future seem to flow over into each other. We are filled from within and we extend to all around us. We experience being the center of the universe. But we know and feel that the universe does not depend on us.

On the contrary, the experience is that often it depends on an outside, transcending power. This realization is for many as fundamental as the awareness that we are the center of the universe. While feeling one with the universe, people realize that there is a domain that surpasses it. It supposes a "somebody or something"—difficult to name—that transcends them, their experience, and in a sense even their universe.

15

I experience that I did not make myself. I know that I have come from somewhere and depend on something. This mystery, which hides behind our universe, can be approached in very different ways to try to "solve" it. It has occasioned much speculation and it caused so much suffering and misery. Think of all the human sacrifices brought about because of this perplexity.

These different interpretations indicate that we have no name for "it," that we have no grip on it. We are helpless before it. An example from everyday life might illustrate our problem. You go for a swim alone in a river you're not familiar with. Your mother told you to never do that, but you do. The river is full of strong undercurrents that you do not expect. Powers much stronger than you are pulling you under. You cannot make it; you are going to drown. Then you see from the river a man working in the field near the riverbank. You see him and you need him very badly. You still have sufficient voice to shout. Not knowing his name, you can only shout, "Help, hey you, help!"

He doesn't look up; Most probably he doesn't hear you. It would help to call him by name. If only you would know his name . . . !

In language with a Germanic root we use the word "god." We use it as a name, but it isn't, really. It literally means the one invoked. It is the one who has no name. It remains a mystery, a something or somebody hidden behind it all, an "it" we have no name for, a something we can only invoke by saying: "Hey, over there!" As long as we don't know the name, we are helpless.

The revelation of that name can only come from over "there." Not knowing that name indicates our dependence. Anyone who knew it would be famous. Those who say they do are making a fortune. They can only make their fortune by not telling the others how to find it, and by saying that they have special contacts, special powers others do not have.

Common Religious Experience

A lot of research has been done on religious experience. In 1965, two sociologists at the University of California at Berkeley, Charles Glock and Rodney Stark, published the results of their study of church members in northern California. One of the questions they asked their random sample of 3000 people was whether they had ever "had a feeling that you were somehow in the presence of God." Forty-five percent of the Protestants and 43 percent of the Catholics said they were "sure" they had, and a further 28 percent of Protestants and 23 percent of Catholics "thought" they had. Overall, more than two-thirds of this group of church members at least "thought" that they had directly experienced God's presence. The two researchers were very surprised, which they didn't hide:

> There are few clues in the culture which would lead an observer to predict so high a rate of supernaturalism in what seems to be an increasingly modern, scientific and secularized society. For example, characters in contemporary literature rarely undergo such encounters with the divine; when they do, it is usually clear that they are odd people, old fashioned, simple, demented and the like.[1]

In 1960, two other sociologists, Kurt Back and Linda Bourque, at Duke University in North Carolina wondered whether ordinary commercial opinion polls could be used to inquire about deep personal matters that might involve strong emotions.[2] In 1962, 1966, and 1967 they put a question on religious experience into ordinary Gallup surveys. "Would you say that you ever had a 'religious or mystical experience,' that is, a moment of sudden religious insight or awakening?"

In 1962, 20.5 percent said yes; in 1966, this rose to nearly 32 percent; in 1967, it was just over 41 percent. At first the two researchers couldn't make sense of it. It was clear from the rest of the survey that people had understood the question. Why was there a steady increase in positive response?

They came to two conclusions. First, around 1967 there was a rising interest in mysticism and religious experience; it was the decade of the search for the mystic revolution. It was almost 1968, that amazing mythical year when so many thought the world was going to change radically. They were the years that the pilgrimage was taken in drugs, and the journey was into Eastern religions.

The other reason was the way the question had been asked. In the 1962 survey there had only been one question on religion, in the second there were three, and in the third, eleven.

There might be a third reason, indicated by the difference they found between Catholics and Protestants. Would the possibility and the eventuality of such a personal spiritual experience have something to do with the hierarchical pattern of the church the surveyed people belonged to?

In 1973, Greeley and McCready collected data that showed that 35 percent of Americans would claim to have had what they called an "ecstatic" experience, the feeling that they had been very close to a powerful spiritual force that seemed to lift them out of themselves.[3] This means that more than fifty million adult Americans believed that they had a religious experience. Research in Great Britain rendered practically the same percentage. Answering the question "Have you ever been aware of or influenced by a presence or a power . . . ?" 36 percent of the people approached by the British National Opinion Poll answered yes. And answering the question the poll had taken over from Greeley and McCready, "Have you ever felt as though you were very close to a powerful spiritual force that seemed to lift you out of yourself?" 31 percent (four percent less than in the United States) answered in the affirmative.[4]

It is interesting to see how the experience is distributed over the different denominations:[5]

Agnostics	23%
Don't Know	23%
Atheists	24%
Anglicans	33%
Jewish	39%
Roman Catholics	41%
Other Non-Christians	60%
Other Christians	68%

Note that the less Christians are bound to a hierarchical, institutionalized church, the more they seem to be open to ecstasy! A hierarchical church leadership always has difficulties with the spiritual experiences of their faithful. The gradual diminishment of the influence of that type of leadership might be another reason why the religious experience seems to be growing. There are good reasons to believe so.

We are starting to better understand why the Gnostic literature in the early church was consistently destroyed. It was eradicated to the extent that we know something about it only through quotations in the the official church writings that attacked it and declared it heretical.

Light From Within

In 1945, Muhammad 'Ali al-Samman Muhammad Khalifah discovered a whole Gnostic library in the Egyptian desert at Nag Hammadi, while digging on his farm. The documents made it clear that the Gnostic Christians emphasized the inner quest for spiritual understanding and that they did not only resist accepting the authority of clergy, pope, bishops, and priests, but also the creed and the New Testament canon, which excluded their sources of spirituality from the official list of inspired books.

Those Gnostic sources offer a different perspective than the gospels we are accustomed to. When in one of the Gnostic documents, *The Dialogue of the Savior*, Jesus is asked, "What is the place we shall go to?" he answers, "The place you can reach, stand there!" And another Gnostic book, *The Gospel of Thomas*, answers the same question with "There is light within a man, and it lights up the whole world. If he does not shine, he is darkness." As Elaine Pagels remarks in her study, *The Gnostic Gospels*, "Far from legitimizing any institution, both sayings direct one instead to oneself — to one's inner capacity to find one's own direction, to the light within."[6]

No wonder the hierarchical church has difficulties with this kind of spiritual democracy. It would mean the end of the spiritual differences between those "in" and those "out," between "women" and "men." It would mean a total change of the leadership role in religious institutions.

It is not our belief in God that alienates us from ourselves, as Karl Marx thought. On the contrary, that belief brings us to ourselves. It is the hierarchical institutionalization of that belief that alienated us one from another, as long as we accept that type of organization and take it for granted.

Expressing It in Words

The descriptions of religious experiences abound, even in the West. One of the simplest follows:

> It was just about dark and I was looking out of the library window over _____. I was aware of everything going on around me, and I felt very alone. But at the same time I was aware of something that was giving me strength and keeping me going . . . protecting me.[7]

We often hear people hint at this kind of experience when they say things like "I know that I am protected!" "I feel that I am watched over; my life can't be in vain." "I felt the overall guidance of God in pulling the threads of our lives together."

This awareness of our reaching of and groping for divinity makes us understand what one is trying to say in talking about or describing such experiences. This insight keeps us interested, makes us wonder. It makes us search for more than just unity with nature, or for our own naked "I" which is one with the universe. If I had no experience of my dependence, if I had no idea of the "cloud of unknowing" surrounding me, I would not have any need to find a name for it or the urge to put it into words. But I have, and this makes me look around, and in myself, for clarification, for a voice to sound, for a light to shine, for someone to come.

Are We Different From Jesus?

The people around Jesus, including his followers, faced the same riddle. They started to suspect him. So much so, that when he once asked them, "Who do you say I am?" Simon Peter spoke up, "You are the Christ, the Son of the living God."[8]

This did not answer their query for a name for God. In his reaction to Peter's answer, however, Jesus gave the name.

"Simon, son of Judah, you are a happy man because it was not flesh and blood that revealed this to you but *my Father* in heaven."[9] According to the research of Edward Schillebeeckx, Jesus did not use the word "father," but "Abba." A remarkable word, as I explained elsewhere.[10] Peter called Jesus, son of God. Reacting to Peter's response, Jesus called God his Father. Afterward, that name Abba would not only be the term Jesus used for his Father; he would extend the use of it to all of us, teaching us to pray, "Our Father . . . !" Are we any different from Jesus? Orthodox Christians believe that Jesus is Lord and Son of God in a unique way. Yet, they too have the text in the only Gnostic document the church handed on to us, in which Jesus does seem to do away with that difference:

> The Jews fetched stones to stone him, so Jesus said to them, "I have done many good works for you to see, works from my Father; for which of these are you stoning me?" The Jews answered him, "We are not stoning you for doing a good work but for blasphemy: you are only a man, and you claim to be God." Jesus answered, "Is it not written in your law, *I said, you are gods?*"[11]

The other Gnostic writings stress this kind of sameness even more. The Gnostic *Gospel of Thomas* relates that as soon as Thomas recognized Jesus in the well-known scene after the resurrection, Jesus told him that they both have received their being from the same source:

> Jesus said, I am not your master. Because you have drunk, you have become drunk from the bubbling stream which I have measured out. . . . He who will drink from my mouth will become as I am: I myself shall become he, and the things that are hidden will be revealed to him.[12]

The impact of Jesus in the West became such that his is often the name given to transcendence itself. Hay describes the feeling of a "divine presence":

> Something woke me up. There was something or somebody by my bed. I wasn't frightened. Within ten minutes the torment I'd felt, for some strange reason left me. I think I

had more peace then than I'd had for a very long time. . . . I have enough knowledge to know that there's somebody there, to know that I need never be so alone again. . . . he decided I needed help.

When asked who "he" was, the respondent said, "Jesus, I suppose."[13]

There is a degree of apprehension in that response. The issue seems not to be solved definitely; the words "I suppose" are used. We need more clarity in this regard.

Waiting for God

One of the many who "waited in patience," as she called it, was the French, rather unorthodox Marxist spiritual author, Simone Weil. Her publisher titled a posthumous collection of her letters and essays *Waiting for God*. In it Weil writes that she never at any moment of her life "sought God." From her adolescence she saw the "problem of God as a problem the data of which could not be obtained here below," and she decided that "the only way of being sure not to reach a wrong solution, which seemed to me the greatest possible evil, was to leave it alone." [14] In 1938, she spent ten days around Holy Week attending all the liturgical services at Solesmes, the Benedictine monastery in France. She loved the "unimaginable beauty of the chanting and the words." She met a young English Catholic there who gave her a poem to read, "Love," written by George Herbert, a seventeenth-century metaphysical poet. She learned the poem by heart and used to recite it often.

I used to think I was merely reciting it as a beautiful poem, but without my knowing it, the recitation had the virtue of a prayer. It was during one of these recitations that . . . Christ himself came down and took possession of me.[15]

What happened to Weil was totally unexpected. She had never foreseen, in her arguments about the insolubility of the problem of God, "the possibility of a real contact, person to person, here below, between a human being and God. I had vaguely heard tell of things of this kind, but I had never believed in them." She had never read any mystical works. She wrote: "God in his mercy had prevented me from the mystics, so that it should be evident to me that I had not invented this absolutely unexpected contact."[16]

The core of her experience was that "Christ has united himself with me, in love." It all happened because he took the initiative.

The Melting and Receding Host

In 1916, a Jesuit priest-scientist, who would later become world famous, was at the frontline in France. His name was Pierre Teilhard de Chardin. Just before the Douamont engagement of October 16 he wrote three stories about experiences that happened to his friend who had just been killed in battle at Verdun. In fact, he is speaking about himself, about his experiences in which an awareness gradually entered his soul "as though at the gradual, jerky raising of a curtain. . . ." It is the time dimension and the development that makes Teilhard's stories so interesting.

The first story is called "The Picture." At that time, he tells us, he often wondered what Christ would look like if he should deign to appear. How would he be dressed? How would he stand out against the objects around him? Would the whole world be changed by Christ's presence? Would everyone and everything become more intense? With those thoughts in mind, he enters a church that has a picture of Christ. He kneels in front of it.

The vision starts while Teilhard looks at Christ. He suddenly notices that the outlines of the figure on the picture start "to melt away."

> When I tried to hold in my gaze the outline of the figure of Christ, it seemed to me to be clearly defined; but then, if I let this effort relax, at once these contours, and the folds in Christ's garment, the luster of his hair and the bloom of his flesh all seemed to merge as it were (though without vanishing away) into the rest of the picture. It was as though

the planes which marked off the figure of Christ from the world surrounding it were melting into a single vibrant surface whereon all demarcations vanished. . . .

The entire universe was vibrant! And yet, when I directed my gaze to particular objects, one by one, I found them still as clearly defined as ever in their undiminished individuality."[17]

The second story, "The Monstrance," also takes place in a church. Teilhard de Chardin kneels before the Blessed Sacrament exposed in a monstrance, looking at the white host. He has the impression that the host is gradually spreading out like a spot of oil on water, but much more swiftly and luminously. He hears a noise "as when the rising tide extends its waves over the world of the algae which tremble and unfold at its approach, or when the burning heather crackles as fire spreads over the heath." The host in its whiteness continues to grow and grow.

Thus in the midst of a great sigh suggestive both of an awakening and of a plaint, the flow of whiteness enveloped me, passed beyond me, overran everything. At the same time everything, though drowned in this whiteness, preserved its proper shape, its own autonomous movement; for the white did not efface the features or change the nature of anything, but penetrated objects at the core of their being, at a level more profound even than their own life. . . .

So, through the mysterious expansion of the host the whole world had become incandescent, had itself become like a single giant host.[18]

The last story, "The Pyx," starts in the frontline trenches where Teilhard has the consecrated host with him in a pyx. He always enjoyed having Christ with him in this way. But now he suddenly feels sad, because although he has the source of all life so near, there is still such a distance. He wished to undo that distance, so he takes the host and consumes it.

Yet, he feels that the host was still outside of him, though it had become being of his being. He tries to purify himself and to concentrate. All in vain. "Still the host always seemed to be ahead of me." Finally, he succeeds in penetrating it more and more deeply, but it is as if he is a stone falling in to a well without a bottom. The center of the host was receding from him as it was drawing him on.

Not being able to reach the host's center, he decides to try to grasp its surface. But each touch produces a new differentiation, a new complexity. Every time he thinks he holds the host, he holds "not the host at all, but one or other of the thousand entities which make up our lives: a suffering, a joy, a task, a friend to love or to console. . . ."[19]

Finally, he understands. All sadness falls away and he realizes that he cannot have the host now; his life has still to be lived for years to come. He cannot yet be united to the fullness. "I was separated by the full extent and the density of the years which still remained to me, to be lived and to be divinized."[20] He could not be one with the reality he depended on, because he had still to work at it in this world and be taken up in an on-going process.

So are we. We are living in a process. We are on a journey.

3

RECENT
SPIRITUAL ADVENTURES

We are all on a journey. All kinds of things have happened to us in the past, but today we are setting out for our future. We experience ourselves as being taken up in a process, going somewhere. Only God knows where. I am not alone on that journey. I am traveling with my community. The whole world is with me. The threads of all our lives are woven together in different ways. Earlier generations followed a similar road, but in a different way, at a different time, in another landscape, at another level. History never repeats itself.

We are all born. We all live with our tensions, relate to one another more or less successfully. We will all pass from here to there. We all will die. History repeats itself. Even though we embody those who have gone before us, in a way, we are nevertheless all different, each one with one's own charism, one's own place and time, one's own role. The same news is heard by all, but it touches you in a different way than it touches me, and yet we are all touched in the same way.

In history, too, each age and process "enfolds" all the other ages and processes that have gone before. Each event contains all the preceding events. History is not a circle. It is a spiral.

We can distinguish at least four stages in our development over the past years. Each one was in the center of interest for some time. Each one led to a special kind of spirituality. Those spiritualities unfolded one after another. These stages, or developments, did not pass by easily. Each became a crisis and led to controversy. Each development generated a new confrontation, and an added polarization.

Development 1: Genetic

We were born in a set family, within a set society with set principles. Our ethnic groups, schools, churches, and religious communities were characterized by an objective and essential (not experiential) approach to life.

Life was socialized and organized by our ancestors from within their experiences. We live today according to models from our past. The same attitude can be found in the scholastic theology and spirituality of the Catholic church; it is no exception. In its scholastic approach, all has been set and defined. The pronouncements of popes and church were and are compared with one another and with the tenets of theologians. Within that set framework, a person could make up his or her own mind about the variations and differentiations in the different schools of thought. One's thought and experience was valid only in so far as it fitted in the set scheme.

If you entered a spiritual community, almost everything was determined and arranged before you came in: the way you dressed, prayed, slept, ate, worked, and lived. There was hardly any place for a personal charism or for a personal history. In this arrangement, dating sometimes from centuries earlier, the orientation was toward the past.

In principle, its essentialism did not take a person's existence into account; its objectivism did not take a person's subjectivity into account. It simply could not. Sometimes this attitude is called "genetic." A person is determined by his or her genesis, by the family, clan, tribe, people, or race he or she is born into.[1]

The polarization of this attitude can lead to terrible consequences, such as Adolf Hitler's National Socialism, the spirituality of the *Deutschen Christen* (the Germanic Christian). He considered his race, his people, and his nation alone as valid and God-willed. He saw Judaism, Marxism, and all other internationalisms as a threat to the pure, Aryan superrace. He simply disposed of the others, millions of them, under the tenets of his doctrine, fascism, a word derived from the Latin *fascis*, meaning bundle, indicating an exclusive group.

His is the same type of social doctrine that led to *apartheid* in South Africa, and to so many, in fact to almost all, other incidents of racism, tribalism, and consequent genocide. It is the possible outcome of any exaggerated chauvinism or patriotism, any flag waving and speaking of one's country or race as *the* chosen nation.

In this point of view, God is an ethnic God. Hitler saw God as a tribal God. For anyone who favors any type of apartheid, even when it is of an ecclesiastical character, God is a tribal God. "Genetically" thinking theologians and preachers often restrict God's salvific work to those who belong to their church, something still done by some television evangelists. Since 1567 this doctrine has been condemned again and again by the Roman Catholic church.

This position on salvation bounced back into vogue as often as it was condemned. It is one of the last officially condemned heresies. In 1953, Rev. P. L. Feeney was excommunicated from the Catholic church because he held this position.

Development 2: Personalistic

By 1945, almost the whole world had organized itself in its fight against Hitler's fascism, which was overcome after a bitter struggle in which millions died. In the euphoria after this victory the Universal Rights of Man was promulgated in 1948. This declaration guaranteed respect for each human person, for his or her personal experiences, subjectivity, and conscience. The respect for the individual person took on a new meaning.

This respect was also due to the developments in the sciences, such as biology, sociology, and psychology. The question was no longer how we reconcile the old with the old,

Thomas with Augustine, Pius XII with Gregory III, but much more, how we reconcile the old with the new.

The new data often contradicted the old, sometimes shockingly, and sometimes humorously. Did not Kruschev think that the traditional image of God's throne in heaven with Jesus Christ at his right would be destroyed by the empirical observations of the astronaut Yuri Gagarin, who twice reported that he saw no evidence of heaven?

Gradually, philosophy and theology started to take a new direction. In the new personalistic and existential approach, the human person became all important. This was true even of our relations with God. The human being ex-sists, that is to say: "stands out," in autonomous existence and reaches out to another. Only in that mutual relationship can we come to our personal fulfillment. My uniqueness has to be taken into account. The gospels are to be read from this point of view. Great attention should be given to the personal encounters, the I-Thou relationships: Jesus and Mary Magdalen, Jesus and the Samaritan woman, Jesus and Peter. The I has to be considered in its own personality, its own history, its own charisms, its own subjectivity. No other way is possible. In that personal type of relationship I meet God face to face. God respects "my face" and I should respect the face of others, as God does mine and theirs.

A new spirituality has developed. It has become very difficult to be a superior in the old way. The uniform dress began to disappear in convents. Personal charisms were taken into consideration. People started to make up their own minds according to their own consciences, instead of blindly obeying objective precepts and rules.

When the Second Vatican Council started in 1962, this personalistic tendency had become so influential that it confronted the older classical scholasticism. Neither of the two tendencies could get a clear victory; it was a draw. There was a compromise, or truce, but without too much enthusiasm from either side. One side did not understand the other. The compromise led to many ambiguities in the Council documents. Even of an essential subject like the church one finds two different definitions: One describes the church as an hierarchical institution, in the scholastic way, and the other as "the pilgrim people of God," a much more open, existential type of definition. It was in this latter spirit that *The New Dutch Catechism*,[2] authorized by the Dutch bishops, was published in 1966 and immediately became a world success.[3] This catechism was personalistic and existential in its approach, but as much as possible it took the scholastic concepts into account.

Rome, however, did not rest until some scholastic additions were made to the original edition of the book on the birth of Jesus, original sin, the eucharist, birth control, the origin of the human race, and the existence of the angels. The Second Vatican Council led to this kind of polarization in the church the world over.

Yet, it was a good thing that neither of these two tendencies won. Neither the scholastic camp nor the personalistic seemed to realize that they were both speaking from a limited experience.[4] The non-resolution of their struggle kept the door open for new developments. Hardly had the two tendencies polarized the church, when a new development started.

Development 3: Liberational

The year 1968 was a special one over the world. In May 1968, the students at the universities in Paris started a revolution. There had been a slow preparation for this, but the upheaval, the protests, would last for about a year. Hippies and flowerchildren had chanted the need for a change, for peace, for brotherhood and sisterhood, for religious experiences. It was the year when experiments with chemicals to induce "altered states of consciousness" were no longer restricted to an elite. Drugs had become accessible to anyone who was interested. The very popular musical *Hair* gave expression to many of those sentiments.

The students' revolution in Paris coincided with incidents in students' circles all over the world. In North America, university buildings were "occupied" by students. There were clashes with police and university staffs. Such activities had repercussions all over the world. The whole existing political, social, and economic structure was threatened.

In many circles there was a general feeling of euphoria. One could visualize an alternative society. Many thought a new world was about to be born.

That year I was lecturing at the Theological Faculty at the University of Tilburg in the Netherlands. On February 18, 1969, the faculty building was occupied by students. They opened a press office and issued many statements.

The protest was against anything the University had been teaching. The main accusation was that the teaching had been "value-less," not so much in the sense that what was taught had no value, though the students thought that was true, but that the teaching had not taken into account the impact of the different subjects on society. A scientist did research on armament without considering what that development would mean for the whole of humanity. He would say, "That is none of my business; I am a scientist." The same was said of the study of law, economy, or any other subject in the curriculum.

Those subjects the students criticized were taught objectively, that is, one taught the economic situation as it "is"; one never wondered about its ethical value, about its oppressiveness, about its effects in terms of human poverty and misery. In the endless discussions at the Theological Faculty the rebels blamed not only the scholastic, but also the personalistic, theology as being bourgeois and abstract.

Such personalistic thinking made abstractions of the structures in society, which were in reality sometimes so oppressive that all personalistic ideals had become unrealistic. It makes sense to think and talk in terms of the existential I-Thou relations only when one belongs to the well-off bourgeois class, making abstraction of the fact that one profits from societal structures that oppresses the greatest part of humanity, plunging them in the most abject deprivation. Even thinking of those beautiful and fulfilling I-Thou relations is impossible, if one is occupied with poverty and misery.

Scholastic theology was obviously no help either. Its ahistorical lack of interest in the existing structures made it a useless tool in view of the new aims set forth. Theology should be busy analyzing society; it should serve the liberation of all those who are oppressed; it should be an instrument to change society. Spirituality would have to have these objectives to be valid and worth pursuing.

This was the start of liberation theology. Since then, all kinds of liberation theologies have sprung up. Their common biblical inspiration is the exodus story. God is the God of the exodus, the liberation of the slaves from oppression in Egypt. God is a God who will not rest before his people are free. Jesus became the great liberator.

Theologians should not only be analyzing the existing structures of society; they should also be active in setting out the new courses to take.

Many theologians started to use Karl Marx's method to come to an analysis of society, starting with an analysis of the economic structures, because those structures determine the realities of life. That did not make them Marxists. According to most of them, Marxism was spoiled by Leninism, the application of Marx's teaching in the oppressive structures in pre- and early revolutionary times in Russia.

Every country had its own liberation theologians, its own liberation theology, and its own liberation spirituality. Their analysis differed from country to country, as the situations differed from society to society. It started more or less officially in 1968 in Peru when Gustavo Gutierrez presented a paper *Hacia una Teologia de la Liberacion* at a meeting of the National Priests Movement. That paper was updated for a presentation at the Consultation on Theology and Development organized by Sodepax in November 1969, in Cartigny, Switzerland, and published as *Notes on a Theology of Liberation*. In 1971, the same line of thought was published in an extensive study, *Teologia de la Liberacion, Perspectivas*.[5]. The English translation of that book, *A Theology of Liberation*, in 1973,[6] became for many in the English-speaking world their introduction to liberation theology, though the North American black theologian James Cone had already published his book, *Black Theology*,[7] in 1970.

Theologians from Brazil, Argentina, Chile, Costa Rica, El Salvadore, Mexico, and Uruguay followed the lead. The new movement did not restrict itself to the Americas. It took root in South Africa and Zaire. It has now spread all over the world.

It stimulated the need to know about those within the oppressed groups: poor, blacks, and women. Another factor to develop within this context was that liberation theology only made sense if it was in real contact with the people to be liberated. It had to start at the grassroots level. The *locus theologicus*, the place to ground theology, could only be among those people. It would be difficult to expect this kind of approach to come from the top, which was too much implicated in the existing situation and too implicated in the oppression itself.

It was important not only to involve the common people in their liberation and to make it really something of their own; they had also to be educated to avoid repeating the same mistakes that caused their oppression in the first place. A real change could not be expected without a total transformation of everyone involved.

The Brazilian educator Paolo Freire[8] developed his "conscientization" method of training for transformation. All over the Third World, people started to apply his method to help the oppressed to find the truth about themselves. According to Freire, it is necessary for oppressed persons to reflect on their own cultural, economic, and social situation and to begin to become masters of their own lives.[9]

Of forty North American education majors interviewed in 1979 at Florida International University in Miami, all admired Freire's method, but the majority thought the method should not be employed because of the political consequences. They thought it better not to let the poor learn the truth about themselves and about the society in which they were trying to survive.[10]

Liberation theology has left hardly anyone untouched, if only because Rome has warned us to be careful about this development. Rome's official reason seems to be its Marxist character, but the real reason might be that conscientization is considered a threat. Conscientization seems to suggest that "truth" is hiding in any human being, and that truth is not the privilege of some who made themselves superior to others. That seems to smack of something the old Gnostics believed.

The new theology, however, gave us a new reason to be polarized. Liberation theologians often cannot understand how a sincere Christian could be in "the other camp." How can you be a Christian in our day, they ask, "without looking for an alternative society? Shouldn't everyone be looking for the Kingdom of God to be realized here on earth?" But some opponents maintain that liberation theologians are preaching only class struggle, revolution, and Marxism.

Since 1969, we have encountered three polarizations in our theological and spiritual world: the scholastic, the personalistic, and the liberation experience. But a new worry started to put the coming of the Kingdom here on earth in serious jeopardy. Our journey had not yet come to an end.

Development 4: Creational

On March 28, 1979, disaster hit the nuclear energy plant at Harrisburg, Pennsylvania. The accident shocked the Western world. Demonstrations protesting the "peaceful use" of nuclear energy were organized everywhere. In December of the same year NATO decided to deploy atomic weapons in Western Europe. A new wave of protest demonstrators marched through the streets of the Western capitals. Never in human history had so many people been brought together in protest. It was a necessary protest because humanity was living on the edge of extinction. At any moment a nuclear disaster might destroy the whole of our environment. Any other polarization did not seem to make much sense. What is the use of fighting over ideologies and theologies when your very existence is threatened, when East and West are stockpiling weapons endlessly.

But that is not the only way we are opting for death. At the moment our lifestyle is spoiling our environment. This pollution of the air, the water, and the earth has taken on such proportions that it could lead us to the end of human life on earth even without an atomic holocaust. Mother Earth seen by the astronauts as so beautifully dressed in blue and white is on the verge of death. We are keeping her and ourselves at death's door.

No wonder, then, that over the earth environmental interest groups and peace movements sprang up.

A new world consciousness started to influence us, an attitude opting for life and not for death. A call to peacemaking was heard. Theologies responded to this new challenge and started to reconsider the meaning of creation. This happened especially where the dangers were very acutely felt, and where a tradition of a philosophy and theology that envisaged *the whole of nature as one life-process* had already developed: the United States. It was a vision dating back to William James and systematized by Alfred North Whitehead.

There are many theories why this type of "organic" thinking originated in this country. One of the explanations is the constant contact Western culture here has had with the "primal" visions of the original inhabitants of North America and the migrated African poplulation later on. These primal visions have very often led to very outspoken views of creation and of our relationship with nature and with our Mother Earth. This creational spirituality found a happy and joyful expression in the work of the Institute of Creation Centered Spirituality of Mundelein College, Chicago, with Matthew Fox, O.P. as its main spokesman.

According to this spirituality, we should no longer force ourselves on nature and on one another by trying to climb higher and higher on the ladder of Jacob. We should give in to, and live with, the soft powers in nature and in ourselves and dance in the circle of Sarah. We should be sensual and prophetic. We should feel at one with nature and live accordingly. We should bring out all our feminine and masculine potentialities. We should make love and not war. We should be faithful to and respectful of our origins. We should live according to our nature. We should be rational and intuitive, using both the right and the left sides of our brain. We should add to the phallic symbol of the cross the womb symbol of the empty tomb, out of which union new life is born.

Although this spirituality must have been influenced by American Indian thinking, which its resembles very much, Fox prefers to trace it back to our medieval Christian tradition, to Meister Eckhart and Hildegarde von Bingen. Hildegarde saw the whole of the universe as a cosmic egg, containing everything, and growing towards fulfilment: "O Holy Spirit, you are the mighty way in which everything that is in the heavens on the earth, and under the earth, is penetrated with connectedness, penetrated with relatedness."[11] Humanity is taken up in a greater "whole" than just humanity itself. Creation provides a place for us, but we have to give creation its place at the risk of destroying ourselves.

Growing Pains

We have been tracing what has happened to us during our generation. We have not yet digested the significance of those events. Our liturature, plays, and films are still recreating them.

A "genetic" approach found a racist climax in Germany in the 1930s. A personalistic and existential reaction in the second half of the 1940s was the welcome outcome. In 1948, the Universal Rights of the human person were officially proclaimed and promulgated. It was the time of existential philosophies, theologies, and spiritualities. In 1968, the student revolts opened the eyes of a bourgeois society to the plight of the non-participants in that society. Liberation theology was born. Ten years later, in 1979, the nuclear and pollution threats to our world caused the greatest mass demonstrations in human history. It was the beginning of creational, process, and ecological reactions.

We have witnessed polarization in many areas, tearing our communities apart: apartheid and human rights, conservatives and progressives, liberation and "traditional" theologians, and ecologists and developers.

Several times we have compared what happened to us with what happened to people who lived long before us. We are not the first to break through the old genetic barriers. The book of Genesis did this in insisting that God is the creator of the whole of humanity. Jesus of Nazareth did this when he told his co-nationals that God was going to be truly worshiped by the whole of humanity, that we should pray "Our Abba" together, that God lets the rain fall (and the sun and moon shine!) over the good and the evil.

Jesus broke through the legal objectivity of the theology

of his community when he declared that man and woman are not created for the law, but just the other way around. And notwithstanding the objective prohibition of the law, he healed sick people because he had compassion on them, on the Sabbath or not.

Abelard and Heloise did it a thousand years later, in their existential and subjective approach to the "essential" and legalistic structures of their time. Jesus opted for the poor and wanted justice done because of his universal vision, but again about a thousand years ago, and a thousand years after Jesus, Hildegarde von Bingen had a creational vision of justice to be done, to the whole of creation.

On our journey, we travel from a genetic to a personalistic outlook, from a personalistic to a more social, and from a more social to a creational outlook, something that should come naturally to us. Initially, the child can only develop within the protection of the family. The growing adolescent is still very much bound to the warmth of the family, but has slowly to become detached from it to come to mature into his or her own personality. Once a person starts to be in contact with wider social groupings and is interested in society, nature is often discovered, and finally returned to. As one in the center of the universe, this person intends to participate in its story.

Our past, present, and future are simultaneously existent in us in all their developments and expressions. What we are to do in this unavoidable tension — and the consequent possible polarizatons — is the subject of the next chapter.

4

TORN APART
AND YET WHOLE

*I*n the beginning, so the Bible tells us in one of its two creation stories, there was only one person, "Adam." To provide companions God created the wild beasts and all the birds of heaven. "Adam" gave them names, making them in that way into pets. None was recognizable as equal. There was nobody to converse with; life remained deadly boring. Even God noticed it. Then God made the human being fall asleep, and made two out of the one: man and woman, different and yet the same. From that moment, those two filled, physically and spiritually, the whole of the universe with a tension that could only be overcome in mutual respect and love. Human life started in their unifying love.

This beautiful story illustrates our human make-up. I recall a student coming to me one day in Nairobi, very excited. He had made a discovery, he said, that was going to change his whole life. When I asked him what the discovery was, his enthusiasm seemed suddenly to cool down, as if he doubted whether it was really much of a discovery. He then told me how he had discovered that we are made up in two's. We have two eyes, two feet, two nostrils, hands, even a male and a female. There are two (or more) of almost everything. He admitted that there were exceptions. We have one liver and one heart, but in a way even these organs are doubled because they have different chambers, different lobes, and so on.

I must have shown that I was not exactly impressed by his discovery. He saw my hesitation, but then he came to his real point. He still had to explain why he thought this "discovery" was going to change his life.

"The point is," and he became excited again, "that you can't see things in perspective with one eye, you can't localize sound with one ear, you can't walk easily on one leg. You need the two to be able to observe all those things. You can't hunt with one eye because you would lack depth perception and too often miss the mark. It is this tension, the difference between the two, that helps you survive."

I started to see what he meant and I understood why this very simple insight was going to change his life. Up to then he had always been wondering what he was going to do with the two different cultural visions he was supposed to live with in his personal life: the philosophy of his own people at home and the Western philosophy he was taught at the university.

It reminded me of the attitude of another Kenyan student who told me, "What they teach me here is okay as long as I'm here, but it is no longer true when I'm at home!" What the student had discovered was that it is easier to see things in perspective when you have two (or more) points of view, that a single-eyed person is not better off than a two-eyed person, that a single-minded person is not better off than a person open to more opinions. This simple insight saved her from schizophrenia. It would, indeed, change her life too. The type of tension she had discovered in herself was no longer a liability; it had become a bonus. She had learned to live in two worlds without losing herself.

Dogmatic Blindness

When facing a variety of viewpoints, we can settle on one and forget the others. Examples of this attitude can be found in any of the four theologies, spiritualities, or visions we have mentioned in Chapter 3. In scholastic theology one studied the Bible, the church Fathers, and the decrees of the councils. At first, all those statements were collected in anthologies.

The important thing was their authority; the more authoritative the statements on a topic, the better. In the twelfth century, one really started to discuss their differences with the help of Aristotelian logic. All the discussions between the different schools of thought remained, however, within the same realm. It fell under the same ultimate authority.

The person doing the reasoning did not count; even his or her personal empirical observations did not count. This was true not only in theology; it was also true in medicine and science. Everything the authorities had said in the past was *objective*; it was untouchable; it was definite. The results of this attitude were sometimes unbelievable, and almost comical.

In 1538, Andreas Vesalius wrote *Tabulae Anatomicae Sex*.[1] He wrote this book, or better, he drew six anatomical drawings after having opened the human body, and he saw that our liver had five lobes. How could he have seen five, since there are only two? He saw them because the current medical dogma was that our liver is constructed like our hand, with five fingers. He saw what he was supposed to see.

In 1628, William Harvey published in Frankfurt-on-Main a small book of about eighty pages that would revolutionize the medical world: *Exercitatio Anatomica de Motu Cordis et Sanguinis in Animalibus*. In that booklet he compared the heart to a pump, which had been invented by that time. As we know, pumps make a noise; they knock, or beat. Therefore, our hearts beat, too. All this is now common knowledge. We feel our own and each other's heartbeat under certain circumstances. We are all accustomed to count the beats through our pulses.

But before William Harvey and his comparison, no physiologist had ever heard the heart beat. They did not hear it beat even years after Harvey's discovery, because the medical world of that time believed that hearts made another sound.

Seven years later in 1635, Emilio Parisano, a Roman doctor living in Venice, wrote a book to refute Harvey's work, *De Cordis et Sanguinis Motu ad Gulielmum Harveum*. In that book Parisiano ridiculed Harvey's discovery. "Who ever heard the heart beat? No one here in Venice ever heard a heartbeat. Maybe it's because we are deaf; in which case we might be able to hear when Harvey lends us his ear."

What they heard in Venice was described by Parisano: When they put their ear to a pillow, they heard the sound of their flowing blood as the soft whisper of a brook. The blood circulation was compared to a river, ever streaming, day in and day out. If Parisano had read medical literature, he might have known that the heart had been heard beating — without reference to a pump — by someone else earlier, Mechtild von Hackeborn. Around 1299 she wrote that in one of her visions her soul embraced the child Jesus, and she heard the beat of his heart, three forceful beats followed by one soft one[2]. Perhaps the Venetians were the only ones who had not heard hearts beat!

The most famous case of such dogmatic blindness combines science and theology. It was the case of Galileo Galilei, who was forbidden to express what he observed. His case has not yet been concluded even yet, because Rome is reinstituting the process against Galilei in order to exonerate him. To exonerate him of what? Is it perhaps to exonerate the church of its dogmatic narrow-mindedness?

Concrete Polarizations

The discussions we have today are different. They are no longer within the realm of a single vision; they are no longer discussions on different opinions within the same school. Theologies and spiritualities are truly different.

When confronting differences, we can take various attitudes. We may accept the fact that we are in a dialectical process, working with a variety of options. Or we can organize ourselves in such a way that we do not accept the reality and the tension of such a dialectical process, opting for only one possibility. In the latter case we speak of a polarization.

The polarizations of recent years are more and more between groups who want to deny each other the right to speak. At the Second Vatican Council the scholastic and personalistic approach split the Fathers of the the council in two camps. One group, the existential, did not recognize the validity of the scholastic faction, whom they labeled conservative, old-fashioned, and on the way out. The scholastic group did not understand the existentialist approach to sacred truth, which, the scholastics felt, was emptied of all meaning. They did not call existentialists progressive, but destructive rebels.

And the polarization went on. Journalists and other out-siders spoke about two camps; their news items for the media sounded like war reports. Later on, some liberation theologians wanted to do away with both tendencies at the council, condemning the two as "bourgeois." Again, some time later, some of the creational, ecological, and peace-supporting factions censured those who were not exclusively interested in the threatening holocaust or the ongoing pollution of the earth.

Different camps started to represent the various visions exclusively. The scholastics opposed the existentialists; the liberation theologians the creational; the scholastics opposed the liberational, creational, and existential, and so on. It became a confrontation between opponents who were over-looking the reality of the situation that was much more complicated than they cared to admit in their over-simplifications. Those representatives of the different factions were not only frequently intolerant of each other; they were even blind to anything from the other camp that didn't fit in with their own line of thought.

Too often we classify and are classified, as representing one point of view. When we would restrict ourselves to any of the four stages of our spiritual journey, as described in Chapter 3, we are unfaithful to ourselves. We restrict ourselves to one period. That is not good.

Such a journey we compared to the psychological growth of a human being in the course of her or his development. It is obvious a child might exaggerate its being bound up with the family, holding to it as his or her only way of survival. We all know of adolescents who for a period overdo their urge to be "themselves" and self-reliant.

The discovery of the real social, economic, and political state of affairs in society has taken the breath away from many engaged, growing adults at their first confrontation with the raw realities of life, for example, that the richer always live off the backs of the poorer. Suddenly faced with

an ecological disaster, like the one at Three Mile Island—not the only one during our lifetime—anyone of us might have been jolted so much that we thought that the only issue was ecological or nuclear survival.

Do not all those issues and experiences belong to us? Shouldn't we honor them all in our personal set-up? Should we not come to a kind of psycho-synthesis, or better a spiritual-synthesis, where they all find their place and play their role. Should our society and our church community not be pluriform, which would broaden our vision and end our fatal polarizations?

My African student had discovered that it is better to see with two eyes than with one. With one eye it becomes difficult to see any perspective. Being focused on only one spirituality makes us lose our perspective on life.

Different Lives After Death

How are we to break through the polarizations and the consequent narrowing of our consciousness? This cannot be done by a kind of syncretism. Some think that it might be possible to take the best of each of the four developmental stages and mix them. In this way they hope to be able to live in peace with everyone. This might be possible as long as we are speaking of different opinions within the same vision, e.g., within scholasticism, where an opinion of St. Thomas Aquinas can be combined with an insight from Duns Scotus. It is not possible when we are working with scholasticism and existentialism, with liberation theology and a creational approach.

These structurally different viewpoints make it impossible to mix the elements. In time we will notice that we are deceiving ourselves if we think the combination is possible; the differences are too fundamental.

Being faithful to ourselves and to our development, we will have to admit that the differences are part of ourselves; they will remain functioning in us. We simply do not know all the answers and have no grip over reality. We are not yet at the end of the road; the Kingdom is not yet settled in us; we are on the way. This tension is part of us.

Each one of the different approaches has its own place in our spiritual and psychological set-up. Sometimes we need one approach, at another time we will need another. It depends on the situation and the need of each moment. This will unavoidably lead to apparent contradictions. Smits[3] illustrates this point when comparing the different answers given to questions on afterlife in two opinion polls in The Netherlands. Asked whether they believed in life after death, 31% answered "Yes, there is life after death"; 37 percent did not know, and 31 percent said: "No, there is no life after death." (One percent answered invalidly.) When asked "Do you believe in your personal life after death?" only 17% answered yes. When asked "Do you think you will see your loved ones after death?" 32 percent answered yes; and when asked "Do you believe in the resurrection of Jesus Christ?" 49 percent answered yes.

Looking at the answers in the group of Catholics participating in this research, the differences were even more surprising. Only 18 percent believe in a personal afterlife; 45 percent believe nevertheless that they will see their beloved ones again, and 72 percent believe in the resurrection of Jesus. How is it possible that 18 percent believe they will not survive after death, and nevertheless think that they will see their beloved ones? And what about the rather massive belief in the resurrection of Jesus? How are we to explain those contradictory answers? Smits suggests that they are due to the different perspectives suggested by the various questions.

The question about one's own personal afterlife is answered from another point of view than the question about the others and the one about Jesus. If I restrict my response to myself in the question about life after death, the feasibility of it causes problems. The same question about the others refers to my physical, phychological, and social contacts with them. The question about Jesus has less to do, in general, with personal experiences and is answered from the scholastic point of view. The belief in one vision is different from the belief in another, hence the apparent contradictions. Yet, each statement corresponded to a truth. The real perspective is only seen when we look from the different points of view. If we take only one point of view, the perspective is lost. The student who answered me "I can believe this at the university, but at home I believe something else" should understand that his perspective is formed by the two different beliefs.

Paradoxical Jesus

We should keep these different points of view — these different theologies, spiritualities, and insights — together in ourselves and in our communities. At one moment we will be "genetic," at another moment "personalistic," here "liberational" and there "creational." We will appear to be contradicting ourselves.

So did Jesus of Nazareth. At one time he says, "Peace, be with you; I repeat, peace be with you! I came to bring you peace!" And then he says, "Don't think that I came to bring you peace; I came to bring you a struggle!"

Here he answers the question: how should we pray, by saying, "Go into your inner room, close the door, and there you will find Abba!" There he answers the same question by praying with the disciples in the open and in public: "Our Abba who art in heaven, hallowed be thy name, thy kingdom come. . . ."

One day he says, "I did not come to undo anything in the law," and he would follow all the prescriptions rigorously, and another day he would state that a human being is more important than the law, and he would heal someone without paying attention to the regulations.

Each one of us is in that type of process. We are all kinds of things at the same time, without being any one of them at the same time. We have to be ourselves, we have to respect ourselves and we have to take care that others do not overrun us. Being ourselves, we have to take others into account so that we don't live at their expense. Struggling with our own growth, we have to assist others in their developing conscience, just as they should help us in that same process. Taking care of our relationships with others, we have to be good stewards on our Mother Earth, for our own sakes and for all those still to be born. We have to remember our past and be faithful to the structures and attitudes that have helped us survive up to now.

No One Name

Some time ago the *Christian Science Monitor* published some verse in which the poet asked, in a more poetic way: "Why do we keep on talking long after we have finished?" The reason is that we never finished! I asked once a friend, who is full of bubbling and creative ideas, why he never wrote a book. I told him, if you don't write those ideas down, they will be forgotten. They will pass like a dream in the night, and end up in oblivion. His answer was that there are already too many books. Of course, there are not too many books.

Why do painters keep on painting? Why do composers continue to compose? Isn't it because of the infinite possibility of giving expression to color, form and sound, ideas, and feelings? Is there one painting that could be called final because it depicted the whole of reality? Is there a piece of music that sang of all humanity's experiences? Is there one book that expressed the final insight in the human riddle? The urge to express oneself will remain with us, because no one expression will ever express us totally.

For the same reason, we will continue to express ourselves in different ways in spiritual and theological matters. No one way is final or definitive. Anyone with a bit of human experience knows it is impossible to express the whole of human experience in one work, in one take, or in one interpretation. We are too large, and so is our human world. We noted already that our words cannot emcompass the reality of God. God has no one name. Whatever we have said, we didn't finish. We will never finish finally expressing ourselves.

It is the same way with a diamond. We turn it in the light of the sun, and try to describe it. At one point it is red, brilliant vermillion red. We shift it a bit and it is blue, bluer than the bluest sky. Now the sun seems to shift, and the blue turns into a rich yellow. Every time we start to describe its color, we have to stop describing it, because the color changed. Who can express all the colors of a diamond? Who can express the final word on God? No one. When we are really convinced of our incapability, then we should also admit that what we say, or what our theologies tell us, about ourselves, others, and God is relative, and that none of our spiritualities or theologies offers fully adequate expression.

We are in progress, on a journey. The fact that we have discovered different steps in our development, resulting in different visions, is in itself already an indication that no one of those steps can be the final word. Anyone who polarizes reality is forcing it into a lie about itself.

But isn't Christ the final answer for those who believe in him? He is, because he is the one who tells us that we should be open. His prayer, "thy Kingdom come," indicates that we are not at the end, that we cannot settle down, as if we have reached our journey's end. His respectful attitude to what is deepest in every human being makes him listen to the name that Abba, our Father, gives to each one of us. It is that openness that he wanted to uncover in each one of us.

One evening at the University of Nairobi in East Africa, a group of students and staff members met to discuss what Jesus meant in their lives. It was a very interesting discussion, especially because some of the participants were first generation Christians. They were not born as Christians, but had later turned to Jesus from a different kind of spiritual background.

The question put to the students was what difference Jesus made in life, and also why they became a Christian? The two questions were intimately related. All kind of suggestions were made. Did we need Jesus to know that God was our creator? Did we need Jesus to tell us that we were God's children? Did we need Jesus to be assured of life after death? Did we need Jesus to organize our family or community life? Did we need Jesus to understand how we should worship, or that we should live an ethical life? The answer to all those questions was that we did not need him for that!

Finally, almost in exasperation, someone said, "Why then did we become Christians?" The answer was the story of the good Samaritan, the story of Jesus' conversation with the Samaritan woman, the story of his healing of the Syro-Phoenician woman, the story of the healing the child of a Roman officer. Jesus taught them to belong to a larger community, to a larger family, to the family of God. They had been restricting their attention and interest only to their own genetic group. Jesus taught them to break out of the group and become more themselves by opening up to others from other cultures and races. He had made them make the journey described in Chapter 3.

The aspiration of the Christian President of Tanzania, Julius Nyerere, was connected with the same kind of experience. He wanted to extend what is possible within the context of one genetic family, or people, to the rest of his nation and in fact to the rest of the world. Did not Jesus want us all to be brothers and sisters, and brothers and sisters who also happen to be friends?

We should not only be unwilling to absolutize our beliefs and options; we should realize that such a polarization does not make sense. Only when we are faithful to our different beliefs and options, reflecting different viewpoints, can we hope to come close to an adequate expression of our human experience. This is similar to what we do in science, where we use a set of different models to get some insight into what is happening, and where the search for a unitive theory never ends. Understanding this, we will be open to our own history and development and be on the lookout for the history, the developments, and the spiritualities of those living in other times, places and cultures.

5

OUR
SPIRITUAL WHOLENESS

When the American Indians met and hosted visitors they would bring out their pipes, sit down with them in a circle and smoke them. In all the ceremonies of the North American Plains Indians the pipe is central. It is like a portable altar, a means of grace for every Indian.[1] Everyone knows what a pipe looks like. The Indian pipe had a red or black bowl, a stem usually made of ashwood, and decorated with ribbons indicating the four directions of space, and with bones taken from sacred animals. These pipes have a symbolic value. They represent the human being in his or her totality, and the universe of which the person is but a reflection. The bowl is the sacred heart, or sacred center, and other parts of the pipe are identified with other parts of us.

As the pipe is filled with the sacred tobacco, prayers are offered to all the powers of the universe, and for the myriad forms of creation, each one of which is represented by a grain of tobacco. The filled pipe is thus Totality, so that when the fire of the Great Spirit is added, a divine sacrifice is enacted in which the universe and man are reabsorbed within the Principle, and become what in reality they are. In mingling his life-breath with the tobacco and the fire through the straight stem of concentration, the man who smokes assists at the sacrifice of the own self, or ego, and is thus aided in realizing the Divine Presence at his own center. Indeed, in the liberation of the smoke, man is further helped in realizing not only that God's presence is within him, but that he and the world are mysteriously plunged into God.[2]

This is a beautiful illustration of what Indians feel and know to be the center of the universe. Not only that. This pipe is called a "peace pipe" for rather obvious reason. Brown remarks that the mysteries of this sacred pipe-smoking are so profound that it is not too much to say that the rite of smoking is for the Indian something similar to Holy Communion for Christians.

> The smoking was always used in establishing a relation-ship, a peace between friends and also enemies. For in smoking the pipe together, each man is aided in remembering his own center, which is now understood to be the center of each man, and of the universe itself.[3]

In this quiet, meditative, and peaceful ceremony, the smoker inhaled and exhaled so as to express the discovery of new depths and possibilities that he or she had made when meeting others. Each meeting of this kind, whether with friends or enemies, is an occasion for meditation. Such a meeting then, is not only considered to be a journey outward, but also a journey inward. Each contact with another person, especially if such a persn belongs to a different culture and consequently to a different spirituality, helps me to understand myself better, just as each development in myself is a further unfolding of myself.

Each painting helps me to see the world and my own possibilities. Each piece of music I enjoy makes me discover the continuous symphony playing within myself. Each story I hear, each play I see, each book I read can reveal to me my own content, my own propensities. Each religious expression is another indication of my own depth and my own binding to the transcendent mystery hiding behind and within it all.

No wonder that when meeting a friend or contacting an enemy, some Indians felt like sitting down, bringing out their pipe—that symbol of themselves—to smoke in peace, digesting and integrating the new self-discoveries made. For us to be able to smoke that pipe, all should be willing to sit in a circle and share it. More often than not, however, that willingness is not forthcoming. Too often we think we have the answer to all the questions; we know it all. Our contact with others does not enrich us. We react in a negative and aggressive way, feeling intuitively that contact with the other would be a danger to our own self-centeredness.

Different Tools

All human beings belong to a culture. They would not have been able to be "humanized" without that kind of human contact. But no culture is capable of expressing the fullness of human life. We have no direct access to that fullness. We can only speak about ourselves, about the universe, and about God via models, symbols, and myths. We have to use that kind of indirect approach, that kind of "detour." All individuals use their own set of symbols and myths to explain life. In any culture there is a collection of those myths and models that the people would use.

Such explanatory "tools" differ from group to group. Certain human groups would react differently to our culture than would those from still another culture, who developed in another way, in another climate, in another geographical setting or in another period. As long as people from one culture is on its own, isolated as it were, it will take its own explanation for granted. It knows no other. While the group survives and probably even enjoys and celebrates life, the explanation behind that way of life seems to be satisfactory. What else could one want? The explanations they have are not just myths, they are the "truth."

The crisis starts when contact is made with another group, carriers of another culture, and tellers of other tales. At first contact, those tales and explanations of others are exotic and strange. They are superstitious and pagan, barbaric and stupid. It takes some time for most of us to begin to understand that the diversity of resulting interpretation has something to do with the partial character of our own insight and experience. Anyone who has ever reflected, if only for a moment, on the unsatisfactory way in which we speak about the Transcendent should know that whatever he or she thinks or says is incomplete, and therefore could, or even should, be completed. We don't have to go into the depth of the divine mystery to understand this. Whenever people meet and talk about the living or the dead, they differ in their interpretations.

The Dutch author Jos Panhuijsen titled one of his best known novels *Anyone Knows Better*.[4] In that novel a husband loses his spouse. Because he never really understood her, he starts to ask people to describe what they thought of her. He comes to the conclusion that each one experienced her differently. Some saw her as pleasantly frivolous, others as very serious and over-inclined to "deep" conversations, some as an optimist, and others still as a pessimist. All of his respondents are correct; their reasons fully support their descriptions. They contradict each other. Each one knows better. There are all kinds of opinions. Finally, he begins to see that they are not real contradictions. Rather, the reality of her person is inexpressible.

It is like this with the reality of ourselves, of the universe, and of God. All our myths and theories, stories and sciences are part of a truth that cannot be fully expressed.

Our Common Mother God

On Palm Sunday 1984, I attended the service at the famous Riverside Church in New York City. During the baptism service, the babies were baptized in front of all those present in a very congenial atmosphere. They were baptized in the name of the Father, the Son, and the Holy Spirit — and the Mother of us all, God.

What are we trying to express by mentioning all those different names: Mother, Father, Son, and Spirit?

We say in Chapter 3 how the transition from "genetic" to personalistic, from personalistic to liberational, and from liberational to creational corresponds to our psychological growth. Have those four names for God anything to do with those four different attitudes? There are many indications that one of the first symbols humanity used to relate to "God" has been the mother symbol.[5] Whenever a baby is born, it relates to its mother in total dependency. It cannot survive without her. The two belong to life almost as one. Only slowly does the child start to differentiate itself from the mother. It is through the mother that the father associates with the child. Some even say that it is difficult for a father to see the beauty of his child without the mother. It is because of the mother saying "You are so good, you are so beautiful, you are so great"—remarks necessary for the baby to develop and grow —that the father can play a motherly role and say the same things.

If we related to God only and exclusively as our Mother, we would remain too dependent on her. That does not mean that God does not remain our Mother. God does, just as our human mother does, though we should grow away from an unhealthy mother-bind when growing up. Mature people are heard to shout or whisper "Mother" when they suddenly face a surprise: "Mother" or "My God!"

The love of a mother corresponds generally to this relationship. She loves her child because her child is hers, life of her life. And even when her children become physically and psychologically independent from her, she will continue to speak of her children as Jesus did, comparing his relationship with the people of Jerusalem to that of a mother: "How often have I longed to gather your children, as a hen gathers her chicks under her wings."[6] He expressed a desire, something he would have liked to do, but he did not do it. The people of Jerusalem could not be treated like babies any more.

At a later stage the parents begin to play a more fatherly role. They say "You shall, and you shall not," making the child aware of his or her own responsibility, nevertheless keeping the child still dependent. Initially there is hardly any argument. What is expected is obedience. In this type of relationship God gave the Judaic people the Ten Commandments. This type of almost blind obedience makes sense only for a certain period. This father-bind will have to develop into an attitude where the child becomes self-responsible. If that development does not take place, something has gone wrong. In July 1985 a sample of the almost 1,000,000 American teenagers who run away each year from their homes was asked why they "escaped." The most frequent answer was "I was tired of being told what to do!" With some reason a Japanese proverb says that there are three disasters in life: hurricanes, earthquakes, and fathers!

Jesus modified the Judaic idea of God being that type of father by calling him "Abba," the name that combines fatherhood and motherhood, as explained above. He also cautioned his listeners about the "authority" of scribes, priests, and Pharisees, who treated them as children, as if they themselves knew nothing and the authority everything. He liberated them from this dependency, referring them to their own spirit and understanding.

The runaway teenagers just mentioned accused their parents of not having started the next stage in their relationship. Parents cannot remain "commanding" for too long. At a certain point they will have to account for their demands. This can only be done when they start relating to their children in a new way, almost as a peer, as an older brother or sister, as a friend, discussing the issues under consideration, taking into account that their growing children have their own valid ideas, insights, and intuitions. Jesus related like that to those who would have liked him to play a domineering father's role.

Mature Disciples

Jesus' followers often imitated him like fan club members. They behaved like children around a beloved teacher or like adolescents around a sports or rock idol, fighting over who should sit next to him, who is going to touch him, and who he loves most. He asked them again and again to make their own decisions, to refer to their own inspirations. He asked them "Who do you think I am?" And when they answered by giving the reactions of others, he told them, "No, I want to know what you feel about me." And when Simon finally answered, Jesus must have amazed him by telling him that he knew because "Abba" had revealed this to Simon Peter. Simon Peter was with God! Finally, Jesus told them—in John's, the most gnostic gospel—"Still, I must tell you the truth: it is for your own good that I am going, because unless I go, the Advocate, the Spirit, will not come to you."[7] Only then would they be able to mature, in his absence.

No one ever left this world as thoroughly as Jesus. He left nothing of himself behind, when ascending into heaven. He did what parents have to do at a certain point of the development of their children. The day will come that they will have to say, "We have taught you everything we thought important. You know our spirit, our way of life. Now, go your own way, make your own decisions, lead your own life. Fare well!"

This gradual development in the relationship between parents and their offspring — mother, father, peer, selfhood — does not mean that they are separate stages that follow each other, one excluding or eradicating the other. There is a chronological sequence, but they remain synchronically with us all the time.

That is what the mystery of the Trinity teaches us. God, "the invoked one," relates to us as Father, Son, and Spirit. These relationships form attitudes that remain with us all our lives, just as they should remain in our relationship with our human parents. We remain sons and daughters of our mothers and fathers, and if all goes well, they become our older brother and sister, our friends, and we remain under the influence of their spirit. We are baptized in those names, in those relationships. In Riverside Church they explicitly added the relationship to God as the Mother of us all. Trinity and more. To be whole, we will have to be faithful to those four relationships. Not a single one, taken on its own, can satisfy our spiritual hunger and thirst. God is not only a Mother, God is not only a Father, God is not only a Sister or Brother, God is not only Spirit in us.

At this point we meet a new tension not only in ourselves or in our own spiritual communities. It is a strain that resembles the one discussed before, originating from our growth from a genetic to a personalistic, from a personalistic to a societal, and from a liberational to a creational attitude. It is the tension we find between the different spiritualities in our world, as they find their expression in our world religions Understanding and experiencing this, we find at the same time a way of relating to them!

We should be able to recognize something of ourselves in all of them. We might even need them to know who we really are! When meeting someone with another religious outlook, the American Indian would take his pipe, fill it, solemnly light it and start to smoke it, finding in himself all the old and new, like that householder in the gospel of Matthew, who "brings out from the storeroom things both new and old."[8]

Action and Reaction

The different existing spiritualities, and especially the post-Christian religious developments, definitely relate to each other historically and dialectically. Jesus reacted to the Judaism of his time. Islam, Protestantism, Bahai, and even an ideology like Marxism did not just start on its own; each related to what had happened before them. They were neither the work of the devil, nor of anti-Christ; they were the result of action and reaction. One extreme calls forth another. One polarization calls forth another.

It might sound blasphemous to many, but when Mohammed wanted Islam to be a correction and improvement of Christianity, he adapted to the people whose prophet he would be. Islam blamed Christians for attaching neither sufficient importance to life in this world, nor to creation. Christians paid insufficient interest to social justice and the equality of all human beings. They laid too great an emphasis on charity. In their view, the Christian churches were not sufficiently open to other religions and spiritualities.

Within the Christian family itself, Protestants reacted against attitudes and dogmas that had been growing within Christianity itself. Wasn't Marxism in its turn a movement aimed at supplanting Judaism and Christianity with a spirituality and religion that would correct their blindness for the many aspects of human life that were neglected and sometimes even exploited by them?

People vote with their feet, and any religion must win adherents by responding to certain needs and therefore be worthy of their attention. We have to resist the inclination to see different religions and ideologies as entities that exist next to, but apart from, each other. We must not see them as unrelated and irrelevant. We rarely pay sufficient attention to their relatedness. That is one of the reasons why our ecumenical or interreligious dialogues often become very difficult and even painful. We hardly ever discuss the real points at issue. We oppose when we should relate. We contradict when we should be looking for common ground.

Our connections and relations, the logic of our common history, its relation to our own individual and communal spiritual journey, the unavoidability of development are things seldom ever touched upon. The result is that our *yes* or *no* makes very little sense in our religious conversations.

Human communities, which under the inspiration of God should serve the whole of humanity on the common journey to wholeness, remain divided and polarized. That is bad enough. But it is a thousand times worse that human communities rarely escape being used by a political and economic leadership that pits them against each other in view of their own, totally different interests. We should not be divided against ourselves. We should remain faithful to all that is within us.

Mission and Self-Discovery

One of the postgraduate Hindu students at the University of Nairobi in Kenya told me how she had passed all the examinations at secondary school level in the subject of Christian Religious Education. She had been studying the whole of the Old and the New Testament, the development of the Christian church, and Christian ethics very thoroughly. Having specialized in the gospel of Luke, she knew more about Jesus than many Christians around her.

She had passed all her examinations very well, and registered at the university where she had continued her study of the Christian religion, one of her majors. While explaining all this to me, she suddenly looked at me and said, "You must be wondering why I didn't become a Christian, being so interested in Jesus?" It was a question you hardly could escape. I asked her why.

"We Hindus believe that the divine spark is present in everyone, though not all are aware of it. Jesus was very aware of it. In him the divine flame was present in a very special way. But that doesn't mean that I feel the need to become a Christian. God's life is in me, as it is in you, as it is in him. Jesus taught me a lot about my divine life!"

I really had something to think about.

In addition to post-Christian spiritual developments, we met with world religions and spiritualities that are called in German *hoch-religionen*, high religions. They are the Asian religions, such as Hinduism, Budhism, and Taoism. In contrast, we find in Europe, Africa, Australia, and in parts of Asia and the Americas the so-called traditional religions. The "high religion" spiritualities are different from ours. They stress other aspects of human life and consciousness. The traditional mystics stress their dependence on God, who created them. The Asian approaches pay special attention to our relationship to the divine godhead, from whom we all flow forth, to whom we return, and in whom we find our dwelling.

Our Christian communities have been in contact with practically all of those spiritualities through their missions to them. The discovery of our common spiritual journey, as described above, touched these missionaries in a very special way. Just as the ecumenical movement was started by missionaries who had experienced the scandal of preaching a divided Christ among people who had never heard of him, the interreligious dialogue was mainly due to them, too. More and more of them came back telling all who would listen that they thought they had learned more than they had taught. Initially, they might have thought they were going to enrich others in a kind of one-way flow, but they experienced that they were enriched as well.

They expected to be on an outer journey, but their contacts with others made them realize that they were on an inner journey too—into themselves. They discovered dimensions in themselves never experienced before. They learned that there were so many more steps on the road to self-discovery.

Making Contact

Jesus had the same type of experience. He grew in consciousness under the influence of those around him. He admired the faith of the Roman officer, who asked him to heal his servant without entering his home, just by one word spoken from a distance. He was amazed at the faith of the Syrophenician woman. He dialogued at the well with a Samaritan woman on spiritual issues. He glorified God when he discovered what was hidden in the hearts of the simple and poor. He made more contact when he sent twelve of his friends to announce the good news. That number must have referred to the twelve tribes of his own people. By sending out the 72 disciples, Jesus further stretched his contact—the number 72 most probably referred to the 72 grandsons of Noach seen in the book of Genesis as the founding fathers of the peoples of the world—and gave new impulse to this movement, which according to the Book of Revelation, will end in an enormous apotheosis when all the nations will come together, *bringing their treasure and their wealth.*[9] Only at that moment will each of us have reached our wholeness. It will be the beginning of the new Jerusalem. Only then will we really be human beings, because we will be *the* human being.

That is what Pierre Teilhard de Chardin saw in his visions in the trenches during the First World War. His cherished vision was the "planetization of humanity," the growing together of all the different insights, gifts, charisms, and potentialities of all human beings from the past, the present, and the future. He "saw" us all growing together into the new human being, to the point of time when "God will be all in all."[10] This is the vision of Jesus.

A Physical Illustration

It might be good to give an example where this "bringing together" of different approaches, this making contact with and being influenced by different cultures and spiritualities, already had practical effects and made world news. First, a concrete example from the field of healing. In her book *The Aquarian Conspiracy*, Marilyn Ferguson notes that in the health field the shift from the old to the new occurs most quickly and most fully (though we have still a long way to go).[11] The definitions of health and sickness depend on our culture, but we could also say on our philosophy and even on our spirituality.

In one of the very first Western medical texts, written by Empedocles, it was made clear that all sicknesses, even epilepsy, which up to then had been considered a "holy" disease sent by the gods, depend on the composition of the human body. A human being was considered like the whole rest of nature, to be made up of atoms. In the beginning, it was believed, there were only four elements: water, air, earth, and fire. Later many more elements were found. Medicine became more and more complicated. But the classical approach to health in the West remained the same: to consider the human being to be one, rather enormous, molecule. If anything is wrong, then it is in the patient's physical or chemical composition. So the doctor either cuts physically, or adds to or subtracts from the chemical composition. One gets injections, pills, powders, draughts, or suppositories. In China a totally different question is at the core of their philosophy. It was a question of *tao* or of harmony. *Tao* means path, law of heaven, inner harmony, ideal, or something similar. Chinese Taoists try to live in harmony with themselves, with others, and with nature. The ideal of this harmony is water, which is always quiet, rests at the lowest possible place, but once disturbed can be an enormous and even devastating power. When someone in China is sick, it is not so much his chemical or physical composition that is disturbed, but the inner and outer harmony.

In an African context, sickness is something else again. The main problem within such a community is how do we survive in the often barren environment we live in. The communal cohesion was the most important issue. Everything depends on how people relate to each other. If somebody is sick, there must be something wrong in his or her relationship with others, with nature, or with the ancestors.

The Westerner, the Chinese, and the African all have the same complaint: a bad stomach; it will be treated differently by the doctors, depending on the culture. In the West the patient will get an operation, or one or another prescription medicine to swallow. In China the doctor will apply acupuncture or moxibustion to restore inner harmony. In Africa the medical treatment will be to establish a better harmony of the sick person with his fellow community members. In all three cases healing can take place. They are all rather restricted in their approach, but are all valid. We now realize that they may complement each other. When they do, it is holistic healing.

A Spiritual Illustration

In North America, parish priests and their associates very often complain that their churches are no longer full on Sundays. Fewer people seem to go to church, though according to the polls that number has leveled off. Church attendance has remained remarkably constant since 1969, when 42 percent of adults attended church or synagogue in a typical week. At the moment it is 40 percent. There has, however, been a decline over the last decades since the high point of 49 percent in 1955 and 1958.[12] In other Western countries the decline has been much more rapid and significant.

The reaction of church leaders to this decline is very often that "people are not religious any more." We have to be careful with a statement like that. We noted in an earlier chapter that statistics seem to indicate that the less church-bound people are, the more personal religious experiences they seem to have. Formerly the church was the only access most people had to some religious and spiritual information. There was no radio, no television, and not even very much literature. If someone wanted to "feed" his or her spiritual life, the only source was going to church.

This whole situation has changed. There are many access points to practically any spiritual information anyone would be in need of. A variety of retreat houses and spiritual centers are available. They revitalize many people. In 1984, Joseph Holland of the Center of Concern said this to the National Assembly of the Conference of Major Superiors of Men:

"Healing the destructiveness of late modern civilization is linked to the recovery of certain fundamental insights from primal culture."[13] And speaking specifically of America he added: "The stronger survival of other indigenous groups, for example, American Indians, is something providential. They are carriers of a different face of God, one from whom we need to seek healing."[14]

But it is not only primal visions that had a revitalizing influence on American Christianity. One of the "secrets" of Thomas Merton's influence on the American spirituality was his contact with Eastern spirituality. Orbis Books of the Maryknoll Fathers has had great influence on spirituality. Its contribution was so stimulating because it came from "outside": from Africa, South America, and Asia. It helped us in our inner journey to discover totally new vistas within us.

The Cosmic Egg

We all experience those different tendencies and forces: acting and reacting, struggling, trying to correct, and to complement each other—slowly growing together in greater unity. We developed these four tendencies in our personal and communal journey. They fill our universe, and we are taken up in the process; we are being born.

Jesus himself spoke in those terms:

I tell you most solemnly, you will be weeping and wailing,
while the world will rejoice;
you will be sorrowful,
but your sorrow will turn to joy.
A woman in childbirth suffers,
because her time has come;
but when she has given birth to the child,
she forgets her suffering in her joy
that a human being has been born into the world.
So it is with you,
you are sad now,
but I shall see you again,
and your hearts will be full of joy,
and that joy no one shall take from you.[15]

Taking over this lead, Paul wrote:

I think that what we suffer in this life can never be compared to the glory, as yet unrevealed, which is waiting for
us. The whole of creation is eagerly waiting for God to
reveal his sons. It was not for any fault on the part of
creation that it was made unable to attain this purpose, it
was made so by God; but creation still retains the hope of
being freed. . . . From the beginning till now, the entire
creation, as we know, has been groaning in the great act of
giving birth; and not only creation, but all of us who possess
the first fruits of the Spirit, we too groan inwardly as we
wait for our bodies to be set free.[16]

No wonder that one of the symbols we still use in the
West to give life to this hope is the egg. At Easter time stores
are full of them. The egg is an age-old symbol of our potentiality, the seed of regeneration, the mystery of life that is developing in a tomb, to be born anew. The egg is a cosmic symbol
that can be found in many traditions, Indian, Egyptian, Druidic, etc.[17] In the egg a secret growth is being hatched. In the
Egyptian Ritual, the universe is termed the "egg conceived in
the hour of the Great One."[18] The vaults in the old Greek
temples, and also in our own church buildings make us look
up to the shell of the egg, out of which we will one day be born
as whole!

When Hildegard von Bingen asked an artist to draw a set
of pictures, mandala, through which she and others would be
able to contemplate what is going on in ourselves and in the
universe—according to her a human being is the image of the
universe, a microcosm of the macrocosm — she also asked for
a picture of the "egg of the Universe."[19] In a fertilized eggshell
all things are connected and developing for the sake of the
whole, for the sake of the being that is going to break out of its
shell. In this regard Hildegard wrote: "God has arranged all
things in the world in consideration of everything else. . . . O
Holy Spirit, you are the mighty way in which everything that
is in the heavens, on the earth, and under the earth is penetrated with connectedness, penetrated with relatedness."[20]

During the growth within an egg, or within a womb, all

the different pieces, as it were, the inherited chromosome elements, for example, are not only growing together, they are also correcting each other. A gene inherited from one partner that could cause a deformation is normally corrected by a healthy gene from the other partner. In a similar way, we hope, the human interaction in the egg of our universe will work. Our over-stressed Western individuality needs something of the old communalism. Similarly, our liberation spirituality is already amending the exaggerations in our personalistic approach. The creational spirituality as developed by Matthew Fox and his school is another example of what may happen when our Western development is influenced by a medieval, more primal approach. We are all in the same egg, growing into wholeness under the influence of the Spirit.

6

OUR INNER STILL POINT

*T*here is another way to keep ourselves together in the midst of all the different tendencies and influences that surround us from within and from without. It is the way toward our inner being; it is the road that leads to God within us. Let us suppose on your own journey through life you picked up the different spiritualities that characterize our generation, from genetic to personal, from personal to liberational, and from liberational to creational. Suppose, too, that you experienced the limitations of those theologies or spiritualities, and that you tried to complement them by your contacts with spiritualities and attitudes that were developed outside of you in other religious and cultural contexts, different from yours. Let us suppose, finally, that you kept all those influences from within and from without together and "whole" in yourself, by considering yourself as a kind of cooking pot, where all these things simmer together. Or, as we suggested at the end of the last chapter, you see yourself like the universe, as a sort of hatching egg, out of which something is about to be born.

Yet, even if all those suppositions are true, and if all those conditions are fulfilled, you will have to admit that you resemble more a cauldron filled with a very complex stew. Since it might prove very difficult to decide from moment to moment, and from situation to situation what to do and what not to do, a "still point," some fixed center or principle, should be found to unify our pluriformity.

Many have found such a still point or an inner principle that has proved to be a significant influence in their lives. Every spirituality, every theology, has a metaphysical aspect, that is to say, a dimension that eludes what we directly see, hear, smell, taste, or touch in our world. It is something mysterious, something coming from within; it is in my heart of hearts, deep in my spirit where I know and feel that I am called by name. It is where God speaks to me in the depth of my being. The Bible is full of those experiences.

Now the boy Samuel was ministering to Yahweh in the presence of Eli; it was rare for Yahweh to speak in those days; visions were uncommon. One day it happened that Eli was lying down in his room. His eyes were beginning to grow dim; he could no longer see. The lamp of the Lord had not yet gone out, and Samuel was lying in the sanctuary of Yahweh where the Ark of God was, when Yahweh called: "Samuel, Samuel!" He answered: "Here I am."

Then he ran to Eli and said: "Here I am, since you called me." Eli said: "I did not call. Go back and lie down." So he went and lay down. Once again Yahweh called: "Samuel, Samuel!" Samuel got up and went to Eli and said: "Here I am, since you called me." He replied, "I did not call you, my son; go back and lie down." Samuel had as yet no knowledge of Yahweh and the word of Yahweh had not yet been revealed to him.

Once again God called, the third time. Samuel got up and went to Eli, and said: "Here I am, since you called me." Eli then understood that it was Yahweh who was calling the boy, and he said to Samuel, "Go and lie down, and if someone calls say, 'Speak, Yahweh, you servant is listening.'" So Samuel went down and lay in his place. Yahweh then came and stood by, calling as he had done before, "Samuel, Samuel!" Samuel answered, "Speak, Yahweh, your servant is listening."[1]

It was in this way that others had been called: "Abram, Abraham!" It was in this way that others would be called: "Mary, Mary!" It is a call each of us hears at the moment God calls our name. There are very many beautiful descriptions in our days of being "named" by God.

Singing in a Concentration Camp

Etty Hillesum was born on January 15, 1914, in the Dutch town of Middelburg. Her father was Dutch, but her mother, Rebecca Bernstein, was a Russian by birth, who had fled to the Netherlands after a massacre in her homeland. Etty studied law, Slavonic languages, and psychology. During her studies in Amsterdam the Second World War broke out. In May 1940, the Nazis occupied the Netherlands, and two years later they organized the first big military raid against the Jews in Amsterdam. Etty volunteered to go with the captured Jews to Westerbork, a halfway concentration camp, where transportation to extermination camps in Germany was organized. She did not want to escape the fate of her people. She wanted to use her strength to bring light into the lives of those who suffered most.

She remained there from August 1942 to September 1943, working in the hospital, but on September 7, 1943, her father, mother, sister, and she were put on a train to Auschwitz. She died on November 30, 1943. On her way to death, she threw a postcard out of the train. The card read: "We left the camp singing!"[2] Etty had kept a diary during the last two years of her life. She wrote: "I would like to feel the contours of these times with my fingertips."[3] That is what she did. Faithful to her people in its immense suffering, she was very aware of her own personal dimensions, of her belonging to the great human wholeness: "I feel a bond with all your warring creatures." On New Year's Eve, 1941, she discovered the possibility of listening to her inner self: "A greater awareness and hence easier access to my inner sources."[4] Soon she understood that what she was doing was really "listening in" to God in her innermost being.

"Hineinhoerchen." I so wish I could find a Dutch equivalent for that German word. Truly, my life is one long hearkening unto myself and unto others, unto God. And if I say that I hearken, it is really God who hearkens inside me. The most essential and the deepest in me is hearkening unto the most essential and deepest in the other.[5]

She experienced that God had a dwelling place in her. Having found this "home" in herself, she is at home everywhere, even in the concentration camp of Westerbork.

I have no nostalgia left. I feel at home. I have learned so much about it here. We *are* at home. Under the sky, in every place on earth, if only we carry everything within us.

I often felt, and I still feel, like a ship with a precious cargo; the moorings have been slipped and now the ship is free to take its load to any place on earth. We must be our own country.[6]

This "listening in" gives her enormous energy. It allows her also to "read" others.

I embark on a slow voyage of exploration with everyone who comes to me. And I thank You for the great gift of being able to read people. Sometimes they seem like houses with open doors. I walk in and roam through passages and rooms, and every house is furnished a little differently and yet they are all of them the same, and everyone must be turned into a dwelling dedicated to You, O God. And I promise You, yes, I promise that I shall try to find a dwelling and a refuge for You in as many houses as possible. There are so many empty houses, and I shall prepare them all for You, the most honored lodger. Please forgive this poor metaphor.[7]

It is because of this experience of God being in everyone and everything that she can even relate to her captors. There is some "eternity" in all. It is her relation to this "inner," to the "mystical moment" in her, that keeps all the contradictory tendencies in her — she is far from being an orthodox "saint" — in balance, and makes her survive spiritually: *"Somewhere there is something inside me that will never desert me again."*[8]

Reading of Etty's journey into her "inner" world is an amazing experience. Forty years ago she seems to have discovered what we are discovering now, a new outlook on reality, an interrelatedness announcing the new period of Aquarius, as some would call it later. "The earth is in me and the sky."[9] "Why not turn the love that cannot be bestowed on another, or on the other sex, into a force that benefits the whole community and that might still be love?"[10] "I love people . . . because in every human being I love something of You."[11]

She herself was aware that she might possibly be a "forerunner":

> I wish I could live for a long time so that one day I may know how to explain it, and if I am not granted that wish, well, then somebody else will perhaps do it, carry on from where my life has been cut short. And that is why I must try to live a good and faithful life to my last breath: so that those who come after me do not have to start all over again and need not face the same difficulties. Isn't that doing something for future generations?[12]

Called by Your Inmost Name

Any person who wants to be faithful to self and to her or his spiritual journey has to do it by working with, and from within, the different spiritual stages she or he goes through. We can look at the world around us from the experience of our own people, our genetic group, our nation, or our church. We can look at it more personally from the viewpoint of our "I-Thou" relationships. We can consider society from the experience of the poor and the oppressed, or from our bond to nature.

The invitations to take those different viewpoints come from within us. They all have their own "metaphysical" depth, or mystical content; they come from where we are most ourselves. In all those instances we are being touched by and touching the same inner being in us.

We relate to our deepest self differently from moment to moment, from situation to situation: sometimes jubilant, sometimes indignant; sometimes legalistic, sometimes charismatic; sometimes pleading for love and understanding, then again for justice.

This invitation to engage in an inward journey has been heard in all spiritualities and theologies and through all the ages. The challenge comes from where God sometimes whispers to us, and at other times shouts at us, from within the boundless spaces within our heart.

These invitations have come from within even during the period when we were taught that we would only find God outside of ourselves, above us in heaven, through the mediation of a hierarchical authority. But God was within us during those days, as God will be forever. God will remain with us even while we develop and shift our spiritual attitudes with the help of spiritual guides, gurus, psychological tools, and religious authorities who come and go, perpetuating and following one another with great regularity.

God remains the same in the heart of each of us, holding us personally and communally together. From deep within us — where God called and calls us by name — we have felt and feel the genetic bond with God, who is and was and remains Mother, who became and becomes and remains our Father, our Brother, our Sister, and our Lover. "What a piece of work is the human person!"

Drinking From Their Own Well

Though all spiritualities come from the same core within us, each speaks it own language. We know that from the past. Ignatius of Loyola, converted while a soldier, and living in a time of growing individualism, saw himself as a soldier companion of Christ. Christ was his commander in the battle against evil in this world, living in the commander's tent in a world seen as a battlefield. He asked his followers to become "companions" of Jesus, willing to fight under Christ's banner. The authority of the pope was very much stressed in his "genetic" and scholastic vision. Living in a church that was often too much structured to her liking, Teresa of Avila described how she found God in the center of a castle after a very long search. Her contemporary, John of the Cross, climbed a mountain in seven stages before he reached the summit.

Every step in our development has its own language, too. The language of our scholastic period resembles the ones of older days. We speak about God residing in heaven. We consider ourselves as travelers on our way to God; we are strangers in this world, on a journey. At the moment of our death our soul will come "home" out there, while our body will be taken up by the earth again. In this viewpoint there are two separate worlds: heaven and earth. God is residing in heaven on a throne. We see "him" as a father figure, majestic and transcendent. When we pray from this point of view, we will have to start by trying to put ourselves in "his" presence, which is very difficult, as anyone who tried will know. It is the image of God Khruschev ridiculed when he said that he had sent Gagarin, the astronaut, out to check whether the stories of priests are true.

> As regards paradise, priests tell us a lot about it. Is it all true? We decided to check, and we sent Yuri Gagarin to have a look. He circled around the world but did not discover anything. So we decided to have another look. Herman Titov went into space and flew around for a full day. Gagarin had not been there for more than an hour, so he might have missed heaven. Titov had a very thorough look, but when he came back he only could confirm what Gagarin has already seen: there is no paradise.[13]

We may laugh at Khruschev and his antiquated concept of God. We might even like to have told him that there are not many God-believers any more who have this image of God. Yet, it is an image that is persistently with us; even nowadays it is often preached to restore or to stress authority in this world and in the church. It is an image that still tells us something we should not overlook: God is our Father, and even if we think of ourselves as an "image of God," we should still pray "Our Father in heaven," as Jesus taught us to do.

We should, however, never forget what Paul said about this prayer and about ourselves praying it: "God has sent the

Spirit of his Son into our hearts: the Spirit that cries, *"Abba!"*[14] Under that "inspiration" we look for God outside ourselves. The call to look for God comes from within! The invitation itself indicated that God lives in the depth of our inmost being. In the final instance, the mystical language used during this stage points at that reality. We are children of God and consequently carriers of divine life. God dwells in us; we are God's dwelling place. God is at home with us.

After the Second Vatican Council the indwelling of God started to be emphasized. We were declared "the People of God." There was a kind of democratizing principle in this; everyone was with Spirit, everyone was a prophet. When Professor Edward Schillebeeckx at the Catholic University in the Netherlands started to stress the general priesthood of all the members of the Christian community, he only drew a logical conclusion.[15] The Roman authorities, however, did not like it, and called him to Rome to censure him for his opinion.

Speaking about God now meant speaking about God in yourself, and about the consequent, very personal I-Thou relationship. It meant speaking about the affirmation of the great self, especially in North America where religious individualism and a personal experience of salvation was often a prerequisite for acceptance as a church member.[16] The awakening of the self, the sure beginning of so many mystical experiences,[17] did not seem to be restricted any more to some "chosen" souls; it became an experience claimed by many. This awareness of the divine-human, I-Thou relationship is a great experience, an enormous step forward, but it also brings its own limitations exactly because it is an inward turn. It might lead, and often did lead, to the culture of a religious narcissism. As Bellah notes, "We have seen a conflict between withdrawal into purely private spirituality and the biblical impetus to see religion as involved with the whole of life."[18] Quoting Parker Palmer, he suggests:

> Perhaps the most important ministry the church can have in the renewal of public life is a "ministry of paradox": not to resist the inward turn of American spirituality on behalf of effective public action, *but to deepen and direct and discipline that inwardness in the light of faith* until God leads us back to a

vision of the public and to faithful action on the public's behalf (italics mine).[19]

The personalistic experience needed a complement. The stress on and the defense of personal human rights has its limits, even in the way Pope John Paul II continuously does this in his encyclicals and talks. Personalistic language cannot express it all. Although the need for the justice that should be done to an individual was growing within the personalistic context, it suddenly started to strike more and more people that no justice at all was done to the exploited and the poor. The majority of humanity lives in a situation in which personal fulfillment is not their first need. Their first worry is to survive in this world. One can only start to worry about the quality of life after having secured life itself. It is only after an "exodus" from their bondage and exploitation that people can come to themselves and *drink from their own wells.*[20]

Liberation theology developed its own language. It laments the status of the poor in an alien land. It speaks about the people of God in search of God's kingdom, about the option for a just human life, and within a church that often has been associated with only the influential and rich, about Jesus' option for the poor.

Two elements become necessary for anyone who takes this new turn on our spiritual journey seriously. We need to understand how society works, how it is structured in ways that favor certain groups and give them an unfair advantage over others, even whey they, the privileged, do not intend to be unjust. We need to be committed to correcting injustices, not just on an *ad hoc* basis but by replacing the unjust structures with ones that are equitable.[21]

The prophet has become the "conscientizer" of aliented humanity, and Jesus the "liberator" of the many oppressed,[22] who are not only the campesinos in Central and South America, or only the Third World poor and oppressed, or only the women and disabled, but also our whole natural environment. We are not only oppressing one another as indivuduals or as groups, we are exploiting the very reality we were born from, and in whose processes we are all taken up: our old and precious Mother Earth.

The renewed interest in our natural environment brought us all the way back to our creation from our mother. This led to reflecting on themes such as compassion, celebration, justice, and the motherhood of humanity. It teaches us respect for the tender forces in nature and in ourselves. It helps us to understand and react to our exclusively masculine approach to ourselves and to one another.[23] We are, after all, conceived from our fertile male and female God. This renewed ecological interest has lit a fire, a divine spark, in us to celebrate the old ecological vision of the earth.[24] "Our principal moral act is to cherish this fire, the source of our transformation, ourselves, our society, our species, and our planet."[25] Without that old vision, humanity will not be able to survive. Our ecological concern speaks again the old mystical language of every traditional native spirituality of every continent. We desperately need that spiritual attitude, just as we need the other stages of our journey.

The Breath of God's Spirit

That original divine spark was buried under the ashes of our past, almost lost. Hardly anyone noticed it any more; hardly anyone was aware of its presence. When Jesus described his role in the world he often used the image of fire. John the Baptizer already did this when he said, "The one who follows me is more powerful than I am. I am not fit to carry his sandals; he will baptize you with the Holy Spirit and fire."[26] And Jesus himself said: "Everyone will be salted with fire."[27] "I have come to bring fire to the earth, and how I wish it were blazing already."[28] This fire was seen resting on the head of each of his followers at Pentecost.[29] It is God's Spirit, God's breath that has set our world aflame again, a flame that enlightens us from within as it did Jesus, a flame that had enlightened many others.

The Mystical Spiral

We have all observed that what happens to us seems to have happened before to others. It is a kind of repetition in history.

This insight is older than our modern vision in which time is like an arrow always moving forward as it should. We have to make progress, to improve, to increase our productivity, to grow.

In the older vision, time was not like that. Time was conceived as a rythym, a circle. This concept is beautifully expressed in Koheleth: There is a time for everything, a time to live and a time to die; a time to build and a time to tear down; a time to hate and a time to love; a time to plant and a time to uproot.

What happens now seems to have happened before. But this is not true. In those primal visions of time, this rythym was understood as a spiral. This is true not only in non-Western cultures, but is seen in an ancient Celtic symbol carved in the rocks of Europe. In a spiral we make the same turns, over and over again, but we make them at a slightly different level: we do not remain at the same spot. We repeat, but in repeating we are at the same time moving up, higher and higher, keeping it all together, and needing all the different stages and spiritualites of the world.

Ancestors and Others

At first sight, it is surprising that we found at the end of our way an insight that corresponds to the oldest known human mystical vision of reality. What our ancestors believed is still in us, an attitude that remains valid. I can relate to what others experience; those experiences are not completely strange to me. I can find them all in me in some respect. An example of this is that we can relate to the Old Testament, understanding that world which was far removed from our present-day vision of the world and God.

The same possibility exists when we are confronted with other spiritualities. We can relate to the mystical flowing forth from a divine and motherly Godhead in Asian religions; we feel we are one with the whole of reality. We should be aware of the riches of the Chinese Tao, the Buddist simplicity, the African integral approach, and all the further riches of human cultures and spiritualities. They all represent moments in a journey we ourselves know from within. We should even be able to place and appreciate the ideological struggle going on in this world between the individualizing West and the more socializing and communalizing East.

The journey we made during our generation was, indeed, made by others before us. But not in exactly the same way, not working with the very same data, not in the same environment. Jesus made the same journey in his time. He did it for the same reason we do. He did it from a mystical moment within himself. He set a clear model.

Jesus' Still Point

Something must have made Jesus decide to leave Nazareth when he was about thirty years old. He went to be baptized by John the Baptizer. When we consider how Jesus normally prepared himself for decisions, this step, too, must have been taken after much reflection and prayer. This practice is mentioned again and again in the gospel of Luke. It makes his gospel different from the others. On the occasion of Jesus' baptism, Matthew reports, "He came up from the water, and suddenly the heavens opened and he saw the Spirit of God descending like a dove and coming down on him."[30] Mark has the same report. Luke is different. Luke writes: "Now when all the people had been baptized, and while Jesus after his own baptism *was at prayer*, the heavens opened and the Holy Spirit descended on him in bodily shape, as a dove."[31] In Luke, Jesus comes to self-awareness in the Spirit during a moment of prayer, fathoming the depth of his inmost being. Filled with the Spirit, he goes to the desert, most probably to meditate upon the consequences of this event. Coming out of the desert, Luke tells us, he is tempted by the devil to use his new power for himself alone, in order to eat, or make money, or to rule, or to be venerated. During his prayer in the desert he had made up his mind. He was not going to see his enlightenment as something for himself only. He starts to preach.

In Nazareth he makes his next move. He announces that he comes as a liberator to introduce the change in society that had been announced by the prohets.

He stood up to read and they handed him the scroll of the prophet Isaiah. Unrolling the scroll he found the place where it is written: The Spirit of the Lord had been given to me, for he has anointed me. He has sent me to bring the good news to the poor, to proclaim liberty to captives, and the blind new sight, to set the downtrodden free, to proclaim the Lord's year of favor.[32]

It is after spending the night in prayer that Jesus chooses his apostles. In such moments of prayer, he must have acquired his facility to see God in all and everything: in the sun, in flowers, children, a pearl, a lost coin, sheep, goats, doves, lamps, fire, water, oil, lillies, men, women, old and young, good and evil, and even in a mustard seed. He tells his parables from within these experiences and visions, using the smallest incidents in the human life around him as carriers of divine wisdom and insight.

During his night prayer he started to experience that his whole world, humanity and all, is interconnected as one living organism growing toward perfection. This process would last until peace and justice would reign, and we would all find ourselves at home with God. It is in those mystical moments that all his tensions were overcome, that he found the unity of his life, that he felt one with God and with everyone around him. It is at those moments in our lives that the Spirit of God is active, setting our spark afire, empowering us for the struggle, making our hearts the loving center of the world, and overcoming polarizations, limits, restrictions, color-blindness, fascism, paralysis, and prejudice. In those mystical moments we are who we really are; the "I" in us takes its place in the un/verse, making our interrelatedness and interdependency real. Although we are on our way, it is as if we have arrived.

The End and the Beginning

In those moments of wholeness, our narrow-mindedness and polarizations, the limits of our concepts and visions are overcome. We no longer restrict ourselves or our spirituality to

one vision, one color, one sound, one smell, or one contact
only. Not feeling restricted by our past, no longer limited to
some I-Thou relationships, not being totally bound to the
option for the oppressed, not frightened by a threat from
nature, we know ourselves to be one with all that was, is, and
will be, one with God.

It was in Holland.
I went with a ferry to Zierikzee
over the water of the Ooster-Schelde.
It was half dark.
The wind was blowing.
It was a soft warm wind that lightly touched
my cheeks.
When I felt the wind blowing over my face,
everything around me seemed to fall away;
only I remained standing there.
It was as if I saw myself standing there,
very wide,
very open,
and I felt myself getting very light,
as if all borders and all burdens fell away,
as if I became one with the water,
and the trees,
and the boat.
I got the feeling that I flowed full of
energy,
and I would be able to manage;
O yes,
I did.

7

MYSTICAL BODY-BUILDING

*T*he belief that God inspires the society we belong to is growing all over the world. It is not a new idea; in a sense, the people in the Old Testament already knew this. They told how in the beginning God blew divine breath into a human being, from whom they and all others would be born. Notwithstanding an ever-recurring feeling of being the chosen people, the Hebrews knew the belief that "we-are-the-only-elected ones" had been undone. The history of the Jewish people began with God's special call of Abram, who was set apart from all others. That special election had been even strengthened by the exodus from Egypt. There were many reasons to see themselves as the only chosen ones. They often considered themselves as such. But at the heart of their tradition and life the Hebrews knew better. They knew that God's Spirit had not only been blown into their nostrils; they knew that it was given to human beings as such, male and female, and not to them alone.

For non-Jews this development is very important. If the Old Testament restricted salvation to the Jewish people alone, it would be impossible for non-Jews to accept such a word as coming from God. People outside the church would have the same difficulty with Christians, if we would tell them—in the name of the God we believe in—that they were not accepted by God. How could a group that considers itself exclusively called by God be indeed inspired by God? Anyone outside the group who would accept something like that would be denying his or her own value and dignity.

When Mohammed, originally called "the prophet of the poor," tried to instill in his own (religiously very confused) people some sound religious principles, he first tried to speak to the Jews. He was rejected. He drew the logical conclusion that the salvation doctrine of the Jews could not be of divine origin and inspiration. It can't be a divine act to accept only one group, after having created all people. According to Mohammed, the Jews must have deviated from the original plan of God.

In his contact with the Christians of his time Mohammed was no more successful. They, too, rejected him and his people. That is why Mohammed decided to develop a new religion, or better, to go back to the original one, in which all people still considered themselves as forming the one *umma*, the one family of God.

Breaking Bread

The Jews had their story of God's universally creative breath from their earliest days. The Christians had their Pentecost experience, when God's Spirit once again descended upon all people, as Peter himself observed at that occasion. Driven by the Holy Spirit, Peter preached to 3000 people. Driven by the same Holy Spirit, all those people recognized themselves in his words and asked to be initiated in the new life that suddenly had become clear to them. They wanted to be baptized. In the description it is obvious that what was happening was a "feast of recognition." Peter spoke in his own language, but the people heard him speak in their own language. His language was of the Spirit, who inspired and animated him, and inspired and animated them, too.

It must have been the type of experience we sometimes have in other circumstances. We sometimes say, "I always thought that, but this is the first time I ever heard it expressed." Peter's words lit up those 3000 people from within their own spiritual lives. They knew from that moment who they should be. The circles they had drawn around themselves had been broken. People became conscious of their unity, of forming the one people of God.

They were not only enlightened, they were also judged. Forgiveness and new life, death and resurrection always go together. So do Spirit and body. Their enlightenment had more than spiritual consequences. Jesus had not left them with a purely spiritual heritage and mission. The very last evening before his passover, he had taken bread from their table, and while breaking it he had told them, "This is my body!" He then took the wine on the table, blessed it, and while handing it around he said, "This is my blood." Before that he had spoken to them about God's Spirit; now he showed them that this Spirit is to have a body. The Spirit wants to be with humanity in flesh and blood.

A First Pattern

The Spirit is variously active throughout the world. The insight or inspiration that we belong together, that pluriformity will defeat chaos, that good will overcome evil, that peace is the highest good, that every human being should come to fulfillment within an organic community, that bread should be broken and wine shared, is growing everywhere.

The development of our communication systems, the still rather rudimentary possibilities that the United Nations and similar organizations offer, are indications of this. The Spirit, however, is not always "caught." Very many are not yet conscious of it. Those first followers of Jesus at Pentecost suddenly became aware of the Spirit; so did the 3000.

From that consciousness an organizational pattern was born that people started to call "church"—derived from the Greek *ecclesia*, meaning "people called together." Within that community of church they tried to realize in two ways the new life they were called to. Inwardly, they tried to form a living community with the church members; outwardly, they tried to spread this pattern in the whole world. They wanted to introduce the new human mode into their own lives and into the lives of others, but they met with much resistance in themselves and in others. Although one "knew" about the new life—everyone had been dreaming about it in innumerable utopias and fairy tales—the still existing old, now outdated mode of life was still very attractive. Coming from within the old situation, the attraction was very strong. "You know what you have; you don't know what you are going to get."

But this new mode of existence, belonging to church, involved more than giving away one's possessions, as that first community in Jerusalem did. It is also about changing oneself. "You know who you are, but not who you are going to become!"

We became accustomed to the old, existing structures and ways of life. We feel at home in them, especially if we belong to those who are on the "right" side, profiting by it. Once at night Nicodemus came to Jesus for some light. Understanding the consequences of belonging to the Kingdom of God that Jesus proclaimed, he asked, "How can a grown man be born? Can he go back into his mother's womb and be born again?"[1]

Nostalgia

In the beginning a new model of daily living was given. The first disciples succeeded for a while in living it. For a moment, there was a very bright light in the dark. But the light of Christian living almost immediately disappeared again in the night. Just as they healed sick people, who got sick again; as some rose from the dead to die again, so the light illumined the darkness for some moments, only to dim again. That darkness, however, was different; it had become more unbearable.

When Jesus left the disciples, the in-between time had started. All the descriptions of those first days tell the same story. Jesus was away, but a new power had been given to believers. Peter said: "Be baptized and receive the Holy Spirit."[2] The Spirit instilled a new attitude that had not been theirs even during Jesus' presence. They were "one in heart and soul," but there was something else: They were one in a corporeal way. They related to each other bodily in a new way.

> The faithful all lived together and owned everything in common; they sold their goods and possessions and shared the proceeds among themselves according to what each needed. They went as a body to the temple every day but met in their houses for the breaking of the bread; they shared their food gladly and generously.[3]

This way of life made such an impression on them that the report is given a second time:

> The whole group of believers was united heart and soul; no one claimed for his own use anything that he had, as everything they owned was held in common. None of their members was ever in want, as all those who owned land and houses would sell them, and bring the money from them, to present it to the apostles; it was then distributed to any member who might be in need.[4]

They prayed together, they ate together, they worked together, they broke bread together, and they lived together. It seemed they had made an evolutionary leap forward in community living. The prototype of what it all would lead to was realized. The attempt failed, first on the individual level: Ananias and Sapphira kept something for themselves, although they said they had given everything away. Peter called it "putting the Spirit of the Lord to the test."[5] Such testing of the Spirit has been going on since then, sometimes consciously, more often unconsciously. In the latter case, the harm is more irreparable than in the former.

Then it failed on the community level. Testing the Spirit, all kinds of "interest groups" started to form along the old ethnic and genetic lines. The report is very telling: "About this time, when the number of disciples was increasing, the Hellenists made a complaint against the Hebrews: in the daily distribution their own widows were overlooked."[6] Paul especially would react so vehemently that one might ask whether he was suffering the same kind of prejudice.

Almost immediately the model of daily living diminished, fell away. From that first moment onward, every believer knew how it really should be. The nostalgia for true Christian living grew. Over the years, in all kinds of ways people tried again and again to realize that pristine living in monasteries and convents, in ethical-political structures and systems, which sometimes were very far from what we would call "church movements." But up to now, we have not been adept enough in handling and following the Spirit's lead. The Spirit has been with us, but has not borne adequate fruit.

The Lack of a Common Need

A group of workers who had been in the Third World had come together to discuss the different transitions they had been going through. They all agreed that the cultural shock caused by their return was even greater than the one they experienced when they arrived in a world that was very new to them. The meeting was full of tension. The common complaint was that nobody "at home" was interested in their experiences. Suddenly one of the workers, licking a huge ice cream cone, burst out in tears. Asked what was wrong, she answered: "I am eating this ice cream, but in Bolivia people are dying of hunger!" They tried to console her, but really did not know what to say to her.

We understood better the real situation in our world. It is one of our crosses and at the same time one of our blessings today: We know more and more what we really need. Also, it is becoming clear that many questions we have been asking are not the essential ones. Very often our problems are hiding the real issues. Speaking about the feeding of the hungry in Africa, for example, might hide the deep structural problems that brought Africa to the situation it is in at the moment. To tackle those structures is quite apart from just sending food and other forms of aid. Fighting for the equal rights of all human beings is different from doing something about the economic inequalities that caused the denial of human rights in the first place. Fighting against voluntary abortions can be done in such a way that the involuntary abortions caused by malnutrition and the unequal distribution of goods is obscured and totally overlooked. Many issues raised in our communities are very important, especially for those who bring them up. Perhaps they would even be important for others if certain other problems were solved first. Many of our problems are the problems of only one group, the well-to-do. They are often "luxury" questions which are of no interest to those who live in misery and squalor. To be preoccupied with our own questions might mean death for the others. We live in our world so minimally aware of our connectedness that we don't even have the same problems or questions. We live in the different parts of the world, in different circumstances, even in different ages. We don't even feel the same needs!

Currants and Corinthians

In 1968, a young girl, Koosje Koster, was arrested in the Kalverstraat, the main shopping street of Amsterdam. What had Koosje done? She had bought a few pounds of dried currants, and was handing out the dried fruit to passers-by. At first people were just curious, but slowly the crowd of onlookers had become larger and larger, until finally the traffic was blocked. Just at that moment the police intervened. She was arrested, brought to the police station, and interrogated. "Why are you doing this?" She answered, "So that at least once people eat out of the same paper bag. They should always do that." Asked why she had chosen currants, she said that the name reminded her of Paul's letter to the Corinthians, in which he asks them to share their food. As in English, the Dutch for currants sounds a bit like Corinthians. The word is *krenten.*

In another town students wanted to demonstrate our lack of solidarity and cohesion. They placed sandwiches on a wooden fence around one of the college buildings. The sandwiches were there for some days, causing mild surprise to passers-by, but nobody touched them, not even the birds. After some days the students added photos to the sandwiches, pictures of starving people from all over the world, Africa, Bangladesh, South America. A few days later, some students stood in front of the fence trying to point out to those who were willing to listen that it is very strange that while people are dying of starvation in other places in the world, those sandwiches on the fence were not touched by anyone, not even by the birds.

In both cases the involved young people wanted to indicate that something has to happen, that our needs are common needs.

In our world there seems to be one underlying human need. We who live in a kind of global state of emergency have to take a step forward and grow away from individualism, fascism, tribalism, nationalism, apartheid, or racism toward a more global cohesion. Our conflicts, political tensions, worries, our stomach ulcers and heart attacks, our hope, and our anxiety all witness to our hesitation and unwillingness to take that step.

Such hesitation and unwillingness are nicely covered over by the intricacies of our daily life, but they are again and again unmasked by our poets, artists, philosophers, and prophets. Of course, it is not a question of only one step. We are taken up in a slow growth, but we have to move on. Born into this world as individuals, our unwillingness to go further seems to be inborn. That is what original sin might be. We have to be rescued from this emergency situation of remaining only individuals. We have to grow together; we will have to form one body.

Jesus made a start. He came when the time was ripe. He came when humanity was sufficiently conscious of its social dimension to be able to understand him. He broke through the old individualistic and genetic human model in a most radical way. He crossed the old human individualistic self-centeredness out on the wood of a cross, showing all of us that this is a human possibility. He finished the old model. A new beginning was made. The new Spirit had come; a new body had been formed. The Spirit that brought them together in Jerusalem made them into one body.

The Eucharist as a Breakthrough

The teenager who distributed currants in the streets of Amsterdam and who made people eat out of the same paper bag, used a model to show what she saw as a necessary development in the future.

We often use models to "have" things we cannot actually have as yet. Children walk around with dolls and with models of cars they hope to possess one day. Architects and engineers use mock-ups to show what the final structure, the house, hospital, church, or high-rise will look like.

One of the many ways we can look at the breaking of the bread Jesus left us is to see it as such a model. The idea is not new. We always prayed in our churches that we, and the world with us, might change into the reality we were celebrating. During those celebrations of the Eucharist people ate together who never would have eaten together in normal circumstances. I remember this very well from my youth. My country was occupied by the Nazis and we boys rightly considered those occupiers our enemies. We dreamed that we would be able to do them all kinds of irreparable harm. And we were willing to do so; it would have been an act of patriotism. Realistically, the harm we could do was not very much. We would walk up behind them and trip them, running away after this heroic feat. We would deflate their tires and steal some bread.

Anyone who was seen eating with our enemies was considered a traitor, a collaborator. There was, however, one exception. Among those Germans there was quite a number of Catholics. They would come to the Sunday service in our parish church. They used to remain in the back of the church, sometimes even with their guns, which they put in a corner of their pews. At the moment of communion they would come to the altar to receive communion, lining up with us. It was a moment when we would not dream of tripping them; when we could eat with them and not be accused of being a collaborator. No priest would ever refuse them communion with Jesus and with us. At that moment all barriers were broken. We were eating together. We formed one family. We formed one body. The future remained future and yet it was realized.

When you go to a building site and ask a carpenter, a concrete mixer, or a bricklayer what they are doing, they will explain whether they are working at an inner, or an outer wall, whether they are working at a doorway or a floor. But when you ask for further details, "What room are you working in now?" or something like that, they will often have no answer. They don't know. They will refer you to the plans or model in the contractor's office. The contractor and the architect know what exactly is happening, and why it is happening.

That's the way it often is in this world. We might have no idea at all what we are really busy with. We might have no idea that we are taken up in a process of growth. But it isn't necessary to know this to be effectively busy. In the description of the end of human history when Matthew depicts Jesus as a judge condemning the evil and praising the good, the latter do not know what Jesus is talking about: "Lord, when did we see you hungry and feed you; or thirsty and gave you drink? When did we see you a stranger and give you welcome; naked and clothe you; sick or in prison and go to see you?"[7]

But it would help if we did know, if we understood. Too many people are frustrated because they have no idea of what is really going on in the world. The idea of a real future is very often lost. Our daily schedules and plans are frequently merely individualistic and personal. Official policies and politics do not reach much further than the interests of our own national or genetic group. We are not thinking, or feeling, or planning globally.

In these circumstances, breaking of the bread should function as a model, which is easily understood and universal in its significance. It is a model we ourselves use every time we invite someone to eat with us. It is only by breaking our bread with others that we form the community we need.

It is our fear that hinders us from doing it globally.

Our Fears

The spontaneous reaction to the idea that we all belong together and should be breaking bread together, forming one body, is our fear that we will lose our individuality, that nothing will be left of us. We are afraid that instead of taking a step forward, we will be going backward to that type of society where the human individual did not count: the ancient primitive collectivity in which nobody was anybody.

The forming of society as "one body" is not completely new. Human beings have lived that way before. In the oldest communities clan members were related to one another in such a way that there was hardly any place for individuality.

There were great advantages in such communities. One broke one's bread in a very concrete way. No one in the clan went hungry as long as one of the clan members had any food. But the limitations of those communities were such that they were only too happy to relax their customs, giving more freedom to individuals. It is not so long ago that most of us left our older rural lifestyle. Notwithstanding our nostalgia for it, we wouldn't like to go back to it. There was a great sense of belonging and security, but there was also too much social control.

Those who talked about the future as living in one global village met with some enthusiasm initially, but that enthusiasm cooled down rapidly. The prospect of living "globally" seemed almost frightening. Yet, at our best moments we remain with the feeling that we all belong together.

> Praying the Our Father,
> I felt a stream going out from myself high up to heaven,
> but then the stream came down
> heaven and earth were combined,
> and bread was broken
> on a common table
> and the whole of humanity ate together,
> because all difficulties had been overcome,
> even those of the past,
> and sitting there I found my place,
> I fitted in,
> as I had never done before.

But even that table creates, or better maintains, a distance. We belong together even more intimately, it seems.

The Distance Left

We are very near to one another while we break our bread and share our wine. But after each candlelight dinner there will be an early breakfast at the beginning of a new day. It is for this reason that we often have difficulty in having breakfast with others. The breakfast table divides us from one another. There we often experience how distant we still are from one another.

It is nice to believe, as very many do, that God came very near to us in Jesus. It is beautiful and edifying to be with God at supper time. It is sobering to realize how far away from us he was. Not farther than any other person, perhaps, but even that is quite a distance.

When we break bread we want to be together. We are no longer thinking only of ourselves, but are opening up to others around us. We are never more willing to be one. At the same time we are never more aware of the distance that separates us. We remain strangers. We are boats that pass each other in the night. In the darkness we hardly see the signals we are sending each other to avoid a collision, a final separation.

At those moments we experience the powerlessness of our human gestures. Our literature is full of that powerlessness. Reading those books is sometimes very disenchanting. More than ever before, we become aware of the distance that separates us. Even the gesture of trying to give of oneself, to give one's heart, is in a sense powerless and hopeless. What seemed to be something touching and personal in the evening is compromised in the morning. Even Jesus did not escape that. The apostles were with him during the Last Supper when he broke bread and shared wine with them; they were no longer with him when he hung on the cross. His disciples thought that they had found everything in him, but he died as someone who remained misunderstood. He warned them and us that it was not going to help that he was our fellow human being, that it would be good if he left us. His created nearness was still too distant.

Jesus was ready to give his heart to them. That is what he

did, according to John. A soldier pierced his heart; water and blood flowed forth from it. But could the gift of his heart help us? The sign of the distance between us was never clearer. The cross is an almost unbearable symbol of our and Jesus' inability to communicate, to be one. Don't we all know it is impossible?

We referred in another chapter to Jesus revealing his heart to Margaret Mary Alacoque. We all know the gesture. We have tried to do the same thing to our loved ones. That is why we know it does not work.

In Jesus someone came very near to us. As a human being he could not give himself totally to others, not even by dying on the cross, though that is the greatest sign of friendship and love, as he himself said. He could give us his bread, and later on we would recognize him in that gesture. As long as that sharing was done in the usual human way, the "communion" both succeeded and failed.

This is what happens when we give something to another to express ourselves. We want to give ourselves, but we give some roses instead, or something for the loved one to eat: a chocolate "kiss" or a meal. But the distance remains. The table we eat at is between us. Even Jesus' eating during that Last Supper did not work. Witness the end of that evening. He showed us that there is no distance in between us, really. He did this in signs. He spoke about us drinking from the water of his Spirit.

It is difficult for us to understand this. We have lost much of our symbolic sensitivity. Yet, what Jesus did is still understandable. John saw with his own eyes that water and blood flowed from Jesus' heart after his death. Jesus himself had once shouted in Jerusalem: "If anyone is thirsty let him come to me! Let anyone come and drink who believes in me. As Scripture says: From his breast shall flow fountains of living water."[8] And John adds, "He was speaking of the Spirit which those who believed in him would receive, for there was no Spirit as yet, because Jesus had not yet been glorified."[9]

What Jesus could not do by being with us and by breaking bread and sharing wine with us, he did by revealing his Spirit in us. After that discovery, it was no longer a question of distance. From then on it would be one inner life in all of us. He showed us how the signs we give one another in our love refer to our oneness, to our belonging together. We have a Spirit in common with Jesus and with one another.

We contact each other materially and bodily, and this makes us one, but this oneness still needs to be expressed, understood, and experienced better. To be aware only of our material reality is fruitless; to be aware only of our spiritual side is also useless. The two are necessary and belong together.

Even in the breaking of bread that he left as a sign, Jesus wanted to express our dual nature. He was very suggestive. With that bread we eat his (and our) "flesh." But after a very difficult discussion in John 6 on the bread he was going to leave to us to be eaten as his flesh, he adds: "It is the spirit that gives life; the flesh has nothing to offer. The words I have spoken to you are spirit and they are life."[10]

The "flesh," the body alone, is of no avail in our human situation; we need the Spirit. The Spirit alone would not be good for us either. Jesus' words were heard only because they were of a material, bodily nature. Without that characteristic we cannot communicate. We would remain strangers forever. There is an other consequence of our material nature: Our communication involves more than our bodies. The vibration of the air around us makes it possible for us to speak and hear. We break bread to manifest our companionship, and material bread is part of the gesture. We sing and dance, we use animals and flowers to express ourselves. Wires and waves connect us with one another and the rest of the universe. In this way we form, so to speak, one living cell.[11] It is the old intuition of the cosmic egg. It is the ancient experience of being and feeling one with nature.

And yet we seem to act as if we are strangers to each other, enemies even, not only of each other, but even of our environment, taxing it as much as we can, beyond its endurance.

8

LOVE

EVER-EXPANDING

S mokers who know about the dangers of nicotine to their health—and even to the health of others—need more than that knowledge and insight to be able to stop smoking. We can be surrounded by data about our needs and the needs of others, about our interdependence, even about our forming one living organism, without this knowledge moving us to do something about these needs. Our spiritual openness to others and our bodily solidarity with them do not seem to motivate us sufficiently. Something else is needed.

Something else is also needed to overcome the fear we described earlier when speaking about our hesitation to give in to our desire to be "linked up" with the universe, to be connected to the others. Notwithstanding our desire for this unity with the universe, our fear of losing ourselves in it often stifles our dynamism. The possibility and desirability of a spiritual openness and of material connectedness is not sufficient. There must be something that should allow us to give in to the attraction that the universe has over us. Is there a point or a moment in human life that makes us overcome our fear of losing ourselves? That allows us to surrender to the reality in us in such way that self-centeredness dissolves? There is: when somebody starts to love. We often say that we "fall" in love at such a moment. Although this expression is used at times with some superficiality, it indicates in fact that something "overcomes" us. Something or someone in the universe leads us out of ourselves. It lures us away from self-centeredness, opens us up, and makes us give in to our deepest inspirations and intuitions; it makes us give ourselves.

Our love poetry is one sign of this mysterious power in us. It is not, however, a poetry that is restricted to those word artists; it is known to everyone. Love is a universal, tremendous, and very mysterious force. It is the explanation of all that grows, of all that is good and noble, of all that exists. It is the dynamic force that unites us to nature, to each other, and to the one—called God—who transcends this world.

We can even know about the importance and power of love in a negative way, seeing all the powers that try to restrict, trivialize, and minimize it. The very people in the past who suppressed the gnostic and Jesus-like insight that each human being has access to divinity, those who today are against any form of "conscientization" have always been eager to point out the dangers of all kinds of love, especially that based on the mutual attraction of the sexes.

They know that a full understanding of love would break the fetters of our self-centeredness. They have made love not only a suspicious and ambiguous sentiment; they have often called it undignified and animal-like. Moralists have often tried to bend love to their rules, but they never advanced very much further than some out-of-date ideas and taboos. The result has been that love often courses though our lives as if it were a negligible factor. It has become almost a parody of itself. "Love" has become the most abused and misused word there is. We ask love to entertain and amuse us. Though attitudes are changing, we still neglect love's incredible power in almost all areas of our lives. It is absent in science, in business, and in politics. Isn't business almost defined as the human activity that doesn't take any form of love into consideration? Isn't that why we say that "business is business"? Isn't that why the main business of the Western world is the manufacture and sale of arms?

Unbounded Growth

In *On Love and Happiness*,[1] an anthology, an editor collected the main ideas of Pierre Teilhard de Chardin on love and its dynamic power. Teilhard's ideas are fascinating. He distinguished several stages. In the beginning, it is hardly recognizable as such. It attracts impersonal powers at the molecular level in the form of fissions and fusions. At a later stage, it becomes recognizable, though it remains at the simple level of reproduction. In the human being it becomes distinct from all other forms of love. It is now no longer only a question of bodily attraction or reproduction. There is more.

> An unbounded and continuous possibility of contact through spirit much more than through body; the play of countless subtle antennae seeking one another in the light and darkness of soul; the pull toward mutual sensibility and completion, in which preoccupation with preserving the species gradually dissolves in the greater intoxication of two people consummating the world. It is in reality the universe that is pressing on, through woman, toward man. The whole question (the vital question for the earth) is that they shall recognize one another.[2]

With these ideas in mind, Teilhard invites us to go downtown at night to see how this enormous human power is dissipated. Pure loss. "How much energy do you think the spirit of the earth loses in a single night?"[3]

Those same night activities can only be explained by the mutual attraction of the sexes. It is so fundamental that a psychologist such as Freud did not hesitate to see it as the force that explains almost all human activities. Teilhard explains this lasting attraction by the desire of man and woman to escape their isolation. They want to thrust forward. They want their inner life to be connected with their outer life.

Love is an adventure, a conquest. It is the lure of the universe we live in and want to be united with. Woman is for man, and man is for woman the sign that neither he nor she is complete on their own. Although they are each the center of the universe, a connection has to be made to live in complete unity with oneself. One has to break through one's individual isolation to be able to make this connection. Only in such a breakthrough and union will they be fully themselves.

This can also be expressed more poetically. "You must be willing to die to yourself in order to live." "You have to give yourself up to be with yourself." "The grain has to fall in the ground and die before it will bear fruit." There must be a thousand ways to express this fundamental truth.

Once the two are united, even that union will prove insufficient. If they enclosed themselves in their relationship, they would exclude all the rest. They would deny themselves the call of the universe. They would be, as it were, a two-person universe. They would still be isolated, not living up to the truth about themselves.

Normally the couple would find its equilibrium in a third being, a child, who is a kind of intruder that beckons them on. Originally, offspring might have been thought the only reason for man and woman to come together. Obviously, it is not the only reason. If the attraction was principally based on the child, then the role and power of love would diminish once this aim was reached, or once the world was populated.

Love doesn't end at that moment; its attraction lasts, and should be explained. Why are woman and man attracted to each other once the possibility of children has passed?

What attracts the two lies deeper than the possibility of having children. It lies in the experiences described in the first chapters: the possiblity of being one with the universe and of being one with the transcendence we depend on. It is a longing for the total center. It lies in the love of two persons preserving and completing their personality. "Then the 'fall forward' . . . begins once more."[4] Love keeps the tension in our cosmic egg alive and effective. It is the attraction of the differences to each other: woman, man, the universe, times, cultures, and transcendence itself.

Woman-Man: Man-Woman

To reiterate what was stated at the beginning of this chapter, one of the difficulties of our time—and in a sense of all times—is that we are afraid to lose our personality through socializing. This fear has to be overcome. We may preach endlessly that it should be overcome, that we belong together and should share our spiritual and material goods, that as long as we do not form an organic unity among ourselves we sin against justice, and so on. But with all that preaching, prophesying, and moralizing, the fear remains. This fear, an existential experience, was behind the Holocaust in the 1940s. It lurks behind apartheid, whether caused by the domination of a white regime, as in South Africa, or of a non-white regime, as in the central African state of Burundi.

This experience of fear makes us arm ourselves and keeps our military and police forces on alert day and night. It will disappear only when we can counterbalance it with another experience: the union found in the love of a man for a woman and of a woman for a man. Their creative union differentiates them, and yet it brings them together in a oneness that is often—and correctly—experienced and described as "out of this world," or "heavenly."

When such connection-in-love is made, harmony seems to be realized and we find ourselves fulfilled and God is with us.

> Love alone is capable of uniting living beings in such a way as to complete and fulfill them, for it alone takes them and joins them by what is deepest in themselves. This is a fact of daily experience. At what moment do lovers come into the most complete possession of themselves if not when they say that they are lost in each other? In truth, does not love every instant achieve all around us, in the couple or the team, the magic feat, the feat reputed to be contradictory, of "personalizing" by totalizing? And if that is what it can achieve daily on a small scale, why should it not repeat this one day on worldwide dimensions.[5]

We experience that we can surrender ourselves endlessly, becoming more ourselves than we ever were before. We know that we can give ourselves boundlessly without losing ourselves. What is possible at this personal level is what we are looking for at a universal level.

Jesus and Man-Woman

John's gospel is considered to be the most spiritual. Some think it so spiritual that they prefer the more matter of fact reports of the other gospels. Yet, John is not as spiritual as that. Describing Jesus' activities, John starts with a marriage at Cana. He is not only a guest, but contributes to the banquet by changing a considerable amount of water into wine. Very good wine, the master of ceremonies has to admit. He came to celebrate the power that had drawn the two together who were marrying.

Later on he would say that what draws us together comes from the Father. That was the explanation he gave of that mysterious force in us that pulls us together. "No one can come to me, unless *Abba* draws him." Without that power we simply would not come together. His presence at this marriage might be seen as a sign. That is what his mother seems to have done, see it as a sign of a possible fulfillment of a prophecy. Together with the rest of the believers in her religious tradition, Mary was sure that one day humanity would be gathered together, pulled from on high. She believed that God would one day lead humanity to a banquet table—so to speak, but that is how they had been speaking for centuries—and marry humanity. Descriptions of that time are full of food and wine, the wine of the fulfillment. Believers like Mary had hoped all their lives for that fulfillment.

Seeing her son at this marrage, she must have thought the time had come. Even the lack of wine in Cana must have been interpreted as a sign. Hadn't humanity been without the promised final wine for too long? So she went to Jesus and said, "They have no wine." He answered, "Woman, why turn to me? My hour has not yet come,"[6] addressing her as if she were humanity itself. Jesus understood her perfectly well. He often would use the same idea of a final banquet himself. In this image the whole of humanity is brought together to be the bride of God. The image is a daring one, but he did not hesitate to use it.

In Matthew's gospel Jesus says several times that the kingdom of heaven is like a wedding feast.[7] In those texts humanity is attracted by God, as two human beings are attracted to each other. This attraction motivates them to do the things they do; it is what brings them together. This attraction is an underlying principle of all energy: love.

Union With All

In Jesus' wedding feast the relation between two human beings is compared to a universal relationship. Isn't the comparison utopian? Isn't he asking for the impossible? Isn't the human capacity to love restricted to one human being or to very few? Can our heart carry beyond that radius? Outside of that radius isn't there room only for cold justice and reason? Teilhard has an answer:

> To that I would answer that if, as you claim, a universal love is impossible, how can we account for that irresistible instinct in our hearts which leads us toward unity whenever and in whatever direction our passions are stirred? A sense of the universe, a sense of the all, the nostalgia which seizes us when confronted by nature, beauty, music— these seem to be an expectation and awareness of a Great Presence.[8]

In other words, the experiences we described in our first chapters give us the answer to Teilhard's question: The "irresistible instinct in our hearts" is born of love.

This love attracts us in two ways. It brings us together with the universe, and it unites us with the one on whom the universe depends. In our Western tradition, those movements are described as two arrows, going in different directions. In that description there is a horizontal movement bringing the universe together, and there is a vertical movement connecting us with transcendent One, with God.

In a more traditional vision, as we saw before, this movement is considered differently; it is seen as a kind of evolutionary spiral. We are moving forward, interconnecting again and again, and more and more, repeating our history, although at a different level, while being attracted forward. We move in a spiral.

Witness to a Global Love

Jesus, in whom our human possibilities are revealed, makes it plain in the gospels that his driving force was love. This love made him what he was: one sent by *Abba*. In this love Jesus was attracted to all of us; in this love the many are attracted to Jesus. Before dying on the cross, he tells us that the true sign of love is the willingness to lay down one's life for friends; in his case, it included his enemies, too.

The cross has been understood in different ways, as a sacrifice asked for by God, just as God once asked for the sacrifice of Abraham's son, Isaac, and as a sacrifice to appease God's wrath. Speaking about it like that makes understanding the cross very difficult. It makes God, who finally told Abraham that he should not offer his oldest son (though that seems to have been the custom in the region where Abraham lived, in view of future blessings), seem like a monster.

Jesus was killed for another reason. He had tried to convince his people and the others he met about their real dimensions, that they shouldn't restrict themselves to their own people, or to themselves, or even to humanity as such. He had tried to take them up in a movement where they—at the height of the spiral of human history where they were living—should switch from a merely genetic and egoistic life to a more universal and altruistic one. They not only refused, they even rejected him. The leaders saw him as a serious danger to the status quo. That was why they arrested and killed him. They did not like his "drawing power"; they did not like his type of love; they did not like him making others aware of who they were and might become.

He made himself a martyr, a witness, to his dream. He died to prove that his dream was possible, that it is possible to be so attracted by one's love for others, that one accepts death for others. He was totally faithful to his own universe in his connection with humanity, nature, and God. He said of himself that he did not lose anything or anyone *Abba* had given him. In this way, he showed that it is possible to break through the old bonds of blood, race, and egoism for the sake of the liberation of others. He showed that he was liberated from those bonds. He showed that it is possible, that it is within our human power, to be liberated in this way.

He would have said what an American saint and mystic, Dorothy Day, used to respond to people who told her, "You're special, you're different; you're a saint! You cannot expect us to be like you!" She would say, "Don't use that excuse. It's a lame one. I'm not any different than you. You're hiding behind yourself! You can do anything I can!"

In fact, Jesus told us the same thing. He even went further, saying that we are sent as he was, and that we would be able to do what he did and even greater things.[9] When we tell stories about his resurrection, we are only saying that we believe in that possibility, too. We are saying that he didn't die when he passed to a new existence, but was taken up. He still lives. He is still with us.

The same passover will be asked of us. There is clear difficulty in growing from a merely self-centered to a universe-centered concept, from an individualistic to a communal approach, but all of us are asked to make the step. One day we will be asked to leave our individualizing material body behind and begin participating in a more social reality. One day we will be all taken up in the one human being who at this moment is "hatched out" in our world. One day the cosmic egg will break open and together we will be humanity. It will mean that we grow together, and break through the limits of race, blood, class, culture, spirituality, and individuality.

This will be a difficult task, yet we can make the step, if we have good will and love our universe. The moment of that transition we call death. How strange that we give that moment that name. Christians call their passover "death," even though they believe we are changed, not destroyed. *Mutatur, non tollitur* (Life is changed; it is not taken away.)

This breakthrough is already asked of us during our lifetime, but we are not yet fully ready; we are unable to make that step completely.

Insofar as we are unwilling to even attempt that step, we are sinful. The total refusal to take that step would be true death. It would leave us in total isolation from all others. If we do not want to open ourselves up, if we do not want to grow, and if we want to fix ourselves in our present state and eat the fruit of eternal life now in the situation we are in, we will experience the moment of our death as an end to everything. "For whosoever will save his life shall lost it; and whosoever will lose his life for my sake shall find it."[10] Jesus broke through that fixation and died (passed) into a new glorified, higher state.

The moment will come when we will make this passover without fear and without what we now call death. Paul tells us that the last ones will not die;[11] they will be taken up just like that. It will be the end of the old earth and the old heavens. It will be a new beginning.

Love as Energy

The love we have been speaking about is a force. It draws people together. It is real and manifests itself in various ways. We are becoming more interconnected day by day. In fact, when we speak about progress, it is often about that aspect of the world we know. It means faster and more efficent communication, which makes us aware of every single human difficulty and pain.

There have always been famines in Africa; there have always been children disappearing in North America; there have always been people oppressed and exploited in Central and South America; there have always been interreligious troubles in Asia; there have always been minorities eradicated and murdered all over the world—but we have not always known that. Now we do. We are informed about what is happening. We are even better informed about what happened to us in the past. Only recently have we started to understand what some prophets and charismatic economists have long been telling us, that our prosperity is gained off the backs of the poor and oppressed. Only now are the poor and oppressed fully understanding that. Only now do we see where loving force is lacking, and where it should lead us. Only now do we start to grasp the breadth, the length, the height, and the depth of the drawing power that has placed us together in this world.

Not that this was never understood before. Paul knew about it.

> If we live by the truth and in love, we shall grow in all ways ... fitted and joined together, every joint adding its own strength, for each separate part to work according to its function. So the body grows until it has built itself up, in love.[12]

Paul spoke about a "spiritual revolution,"[13] about the fact that we "are all parts of one another."[14] Paul saw all this because of his contact with Jesus. It was Jesus—Paul almost always calls him Christ—who revealed by his life and his death that all "share in the same inheritance" and that "we are parts of the same body."[15] Paul is not the only one to see this.

There are many contemporaries who see the same. Even someone who initially did not believe in the possibility of healthy human contacts, Jean Paul Sartre, wrote toward the end of his life about "being outside of oneself in the other," about "the fusion of human individuals in a hyper-organism, as the future that should be realized as soon as we are assembled together." C.J. Jung suggested that the only acceptable modern idea of God is the Spirit, who is in all and everyone, assembling them together. We just considered Teilhard's position, and we could mention many other names, especially if we included the Eastern masters who already have an influence in the West.[16] It is not, however, our intention to appeal to the authority of others only. All of us have had this vision in our moments of ecstasy, when feeling one with nature, with another, with others, or with the transcendent One.

Serendipity as the Test

Behind all this there is that drawing force, that attraction we called cosmic love. If that is true, we might be able to test it. This is not a new idea, only a very normal development. Ignatius of Loyola was driven by the idea of fighting for the fulfillment of God's plan in this world. Being a soldier, he thought in terms of a war. How do you know you're fighting on the right side? How do you discern whether you're making the right choices in life? How do you know whether you're marching in the direction the commander wants you to go? To be able to make such discernments, he laid down certain rules. He did not make them up; he found them in the order of things.

If there is a plan, if there is transcendent power, I will feel at ease and happy only when I am working and living according to the directions of that power. That is in the logic of things. Consequently, I will have to look for signals given to me while I'm proceeding. If I go in a direction where all is against me, where nothing succeeds, where the only effect of my activity is disaster, I am obviously moving in the wrong direction. If, on the contrary, I go in the direction that makes me feel good and happy, satisfied and stimulated, I am on the right path.

The idea is not new. How could it be, since people have been moving toward their destiny for so very long.

It is an idea, however, that recently got a new name: serendipity, which has been defined in different ways.[17] In his bestselling book, *The Road Less Traveled*, M. Scott Peck[18] uses this definition from a dictionary: "The gift of finding valuable or agreeable things not sought for." Peck gives some striking examples; for instance, how he got a book, completely unknown to him, exactly at the moment he needed its message to be able to continue the book he was working on. He calls this "grace."

This serendipity was even more. It was also an indication that what he was doing was on the right path, in the right direction. Everyone knows examples of this kind of coincidences and "synchronicities." They abound in the lives of saints. When in cash difficulties, a benefactor turns up with exactly the amount needed. They called it providence.

If you go "with the movement" friends will turn up at the right time, the right books will almost jump in your direction from the library or bookshop shelves. You sit down, pick up a piece of paper, and find the idea you needed at that very moment. In these outward events we can find the signals for whether we go right or wrong. This is not only true in our personal life; it is also true in our "public" life. If a society does not organize itself so as to be inclusive of all citizens, but exclusive, developments around us will signal that we are going in the wrong direction.

Our lack of respect for our environment is crying out to heaven and to us in its misery. Our land is no longer fertile, our water spoiled, and our air poisoned. Our neglect of the poor and downtrodden makes our educational system and our health care unworkable, not only for them but even for us. The apartheid in South Africa is leading to destruction, violence, hatred, and death. Our competitive culture makes the lives of so many people miserable.

That misery and suffering is not lost. Our pain and the pain of others is never lost. Is it not because of the tremendous suffering of the Jewish people during the Holocaust that we are reviewing all of our human and religious relations. Was it not their pain that made it clear that we can live no longer with a racist outlook on reality? Was it not the suffering of the campesinos in Central America that made us aware that the cultivation of our individuality is only "bourgeois" and invalid? Was it not the suffering of a poisoned environment that made us look back on our neglected Mother Earth? Pain is never lost.

Was it not the suffering of Jesus on the cross that is changing the whole world? But it remains pain.

When we are on the right path, the signals of approval will come from all over. It is a truth as old as humanity. It is the mystery behind all the miracles in this world. It is the sign of blessing. Paul expressed it this way: "We know that by turning everything to their good God cooperates with all those who love him."[19]

This cooperation from without will be the sign of being on the right path. It will become the story of our lives, but it may not happen all at once. We have still to struggle toward the final outcome, just as Teilhard could not get hold of the center of the host he was struggling with at the front line in France.[20]

We cannot yet live as if we are at the end of the path. The new human being has not yet been born. Its birth is not yet a fact; the egg has not yet hatched. The final alleluia cannot yet be sung, but that does not mean that it cannot yet be sung at all. Aren't we setting its tune? Aren't we approaching our goal?

9

CELEBRATING:

THE FINAL AIM

O n a train to Washington D.C. I overheard a man who had just been in New York City telling someone about his stay there. He was asked what he had liked most in New York, and what he would suggest doing there. He spoke enthusiastically about the things he had done and seen there, but the climax had been, he said, his visit to the best nightclub in Manhattan.

He explained how everything was just right there and well worth the twenty dollars cover charge. He tried to describe colors, the music, the atmosphere, but he said finally, "Impossible, but it's like what I would imagine heaven to be, one gigantic feast!"[1] Our final destiny is often visualized like that: an eternal feast. The Bible uses images and symbols like that to describe the final outcome. In the Book of Revelation it is described as a place where injustice is banned, where no one will ever weep again, where we will celebrate a wedding feast, where our laughter will sound through the streets and squares, where the dancing has just been started, and where the best wine is going to be poured in abundance.

As children we were told that heaven would be an endless feast, where we would eat the most exotic and finest foods from golden plates, including rice pudding with raisins. Work and school days would be over. There would be singing and dancing, the brilliant sun and splashing water, green trees full of bananas and oranges and pears, a blue sky, birds, butterflies, animals to play with, all our friends, and even God. The description was one of an eternal harmony: earth, nature, humanity, and God. An eternal feast, an everlasting celebration. Such a description seems to fill in the mystical experiences described in our first chapters.

Long Live the Past

The most common way we interrupt the daily routine of life is by celebrating feasts. Our Christian ancestors lived their communal life from Christmas to Easter, from Easter to Pentecost, from Pentecost to Christmas. In their more private lives the celebration of birth, marriage, and the get together at funerals broke through the usual treadmill of daily life. Even in our businesslike and un-symbolic modern society much of these celebrations remain: Christmas, Easter, Independence Day, Labor Day, the rest of our annual holidays, and weekends, when life is supposed to be at its best. All these days promise a better alternative to our daily lives.

The abundance of such occasions and holidays seem to be the reason that our feasts have diminished in value. This devaluation is perhaps one of the reasons our interest in heaven has dwindled. It has become difficult to celebrate a real feast, which is often reduced to giving a party. A party is not a feast, notwithstanding all the money spent on exquisite wines and rare foods.

More is needed than that to truly celebrate a feast. Certain conditions have to be fulfilled, which are still traceable, even in the feasts we have. A celebration never takes place without a reason. We have to celebrate *something*. There is a relationship to something that happened in the past which is so important that it is a sufficient reason to interrupt the routine of our daily life. That something can be a birth or the passing of an exam. It is always an event that influenced someone so much that she or he is now in a different—and better—position than before.

Every feast has something of a breakthrough, a liberation.

The event need not have taken place just before its celebration; it might have happened long ago. We don't only celebrate birthdays at the moment of birth; we do it long afterward. There is no feast without that relationship to the recent, or the distant, event. A feast is always a commemoration. We go back in time to reconsider a significant event in our lives, to understand its significance, and to experience again the joy it caused and causes.

The Present Future Promise

Some people insist that there is nothing new under the sun, and they even appeal to the Bible to justify this position. There is a similar outlook in Africa. The East African theologian John Mbiti is of the opinion that Africans, in general, have no idea of a real future.[2] For them, he says, the future depends completely on what they know of the past. What happened in the past will happen again. The market will be open on Wednesday because up to now it has always been open on Wednesdays.

Whatever we think of this old, traditional concept, one thing is clear: there is a bond in the present from the past into the future. Even if we believe in the possibility of something really new in the future, we would not be able to describe it except with data derived from our past. We have no other data.

Celebration has something to do with the future. A feast commemorates *now* the recent or the far-off past in view of the future. That future holds promise for us because of what has happened in the past. The liberation will then be repeated. It repeats itself even while we celebrate, because we are "free" enough to be able to do exactly that. If we don't expect anything from the future, there doesn't seem to be any reason to celebrate. A celebration keeps the time—past, present, and future—together.

The More the Merrier

You can't celebrate a feast alone. It is possible to give oneself a treat, but that is about all. A celebration is a social activity requiring us to invite others to be co-celebrants. In fairy tales and even in Jesus' parables, messengers are sent out to invite guests with whom the host wants to share happiness. Not to share it only brings misfortune. That becomes obvious when everything is ready for the feast and no one comes. There is no food more bitter than the food left over because no one came, no drink more sour than the drink that remained untouched. The joy has to be shared by everyone.

Yet, invitations sometimes have to follow a pattern, so strict and formal that sometimes it almost takes all the joy away. Normally, however, there is always a period when everyone is welcome, the reception open. The more natural and human a feast is, the longer that period lasts. All are welcome, young and old, rich and poor. In up-country Africa, no one is ever turned away. The more the merrier!

In Western countries that is still true of our popular and religious celebrations. When those feasts are celebrated well, according to the nature of the feasts themselves, everyone is welcome. In those cases, aren't we celebrating events that touched the whole of the population and, in fact, the whole of humanity? Aren't we celebrating our wholeness, the saving brother and sisterhood, our connectedness itself.

A feast is a statement that human happiness will only be found in togetherness, in community. The celebration opens up the small circle of daily needs and worries. The individual or the smaller group is connected to the greater totality, the community. For a moment, for the duration of the feast, we break through restrictions and limitations. Our desire for a common happiness is fulfilled for the duration of the feast. The future seems to be fulfilled. The end seems to have come. The final community is realized. If only it could last forever.

Yet, after each festive supper there will be again a breakfast with its divisiveness. When the breakfast table—everyone looking at the television morning news or sitting behind a morning paper, eating one's cereal—dominates again, the open circle is closed. The feast, the celebration is over.

The Filled Table

The food-filled table belongs to a feast. Without it, a feast is unimaginable. Eating and drinking is essential for the festive celebration. The fact that we would like to be together cannot be expressed in a clearer way, neither by a handshake or by a pat on the shoulder, or even by dancing. By eating and drinking together we support one another in solidarity. Every celebration creates in this way the atmosphere of togetherness, of mutual security and fellowship. Human connections can be made only through our bodies; only through our bodies can we understand and reach one another. Food and drink enhance our human bond; to eat and drink together is a sign that we are of the same substance, of the same flesh.

Such togetherness, however, lasts only during the celebration. We don't as yet find this level of sharing in our daily life. Normally, we don't break bread together. In the hectic pace of daily life eating together can only be done in a very limited circle, and only from time to time.

Every celebration is a new start. It is an occasion for renewed relationships, new hope, and a new beginning. Without that common hope, without that shared nostalgia, we can't sit around the same table. And these sentiments need to be expressed.

The Banquet Speech

During every important celebration there should be a speaker who has been carefully selected. When no one has been named speaker, it becomes very obvious that the feast needs one. The felt need arises during the feast. "Isn't someone going to say something?" "Why don't you say a few words. You're the oldest." A jacket is buttoned. The speaker stands up. There is a speech. Unavoidably. Necessarily.

The celebration has to be interpreted. (Every celebration is a learning occasion.) First the celebrated person or the celebrated event is described. An appeal follows, an invitation to all to commemorate and celebrate in such a way that inspiration and initiative will be found to continue in the spirit of the celebration when the festivities are over.

From an educational point of view, a feast is very important. The successful celebration inspires everyone to carry on with the spirit there was in the beginning. During the celebration the participants are reminded of their responsibilities; every commemoration places before us again our task in society. A well-celebrated festive commemoration, even of a simple thing like a birthday, teaches more than lessons. It returns the hosts and the guests to society in a recommitted and refreshed way.

A celebration is an occasion to come together, to know one another better, to be more united, and to experience in that way what life in the future can be and should be. At a celebration we break through the bitterness the past might have caused us. Feasting together leads us to forgiveness; it heals our wounds. That is to say, it might do all that, if certain conditions are fulfilled.

Peace Needed

Not everyone can celebrate. It is difficult for the pessimist and the sulk. It is impossible for those who have lost hope in humanity. Pessimists are never welcome guests. If these people are at the celebration, they don't participate. They are likely to spoil the festivities for the others.

To celebrate, a certain contentment is needed, a kind of fundamental accord with life. If anyone has anything against life, it is impossible to celebrate it. It would go against all he or she feels.

A celebration has something to do with hope, which can be based only on trust and confidence. Confidence in the future makes it possible to believe that there are powers at work that will lead to a fulfilling outcome. The celebration is made possible by our belief in the possibility to break through the dark of the night, through fate, and even through death. Each celebration commemorates the fact that human beings are not victims of a blind fate, that we will overcome because we have overcome before. National holidays commemorate patriots, victories, liberations, declarations of independence; family feasts celebrate births, marriages, healings, successes; Christian feasts commemorate Jesus' victory over death and sin; and the celebrants honor and commemorate the heroes who took part in these victories. There is no feast without belief in a victory. Only in that belief can merrymaking start.

Merrymaking

Notwithstanding the serious character of any celebration, the most striking feature about a feast is its joy and merrymaking. This is why we like a feast. Young and old count the days that still separate them from the feast day. Finally the period of celebration starts, sometimes after endless preparations. Daily work and even daily life come to a rest. Everything switches into a high gear. There is music, dancing, fireworks, competitions, games, everything. There is more drinking and eating, gifts are given and compliments made, contacts are forged or renewed, there is much talking and singing and remembering.

A feast is a breather, an oasis in the desert of our life. It can be more fulfilling than any other moment of our lives. While celebrating, we put off what we were worried about. Our sighing and groaning, our work and fears seem to be over, at least for as long as the feast lasts.

The success of a feast depends on the joy it gives us. Everyone should contribute to it by their participation, their friendliness and openness. To join a feast brings that obligation. Only those who want to be with the others and stress the positive in life can truly join in the celebration. To be together in that way is what a feast is.

We need feasts for many reasons. It is only in those celebrations that we know what it means to live human life; it is only in those feasts that we can be aware of ourselves and of our tasks.

A Feast Liberates

Our life and our work tend to isolate us. Our daily needs, worries, and contacts lock us up as in a cocoon. The older French existentialists described this very well: "To rise, to eat, to take the bus, to work four hours, to eat, to work four hours, to take the bus, to eat, to kiss, to go to bed, to rise, to eat, to take the bus. . . . Monday, Tuesday, Wednesday . . . always in the same rhythm, one week, a second week. . . ." We do that for some time without too much harm. Often we don't know better; we get used to it. But then it starts to eat at us; it does not offer any fresh perspective or relief; it enslaves us. This is true not only of our work; it is the same for our family, our free time, school, and church.

There are different ways to escape from this hold on us. Some try to shed the scales from their eyes by writing poetry, by meditating, by praying, by exercising. The best way to escape from the often suffocating narrowness of home-, garden-, and kitchen-mentality is a well-prepared feast. To celebrate a feast is a liberation from the routine of our family, business, school, or religious community. Different celebrations will have a different character, but fundamentally they always have something to do with an "exodus."

A commemoration is a grateful remembrance of a "liberation" that happened to us, in some way. In the commemoration the daily routine of life is broken through, and the future opens itself to us.

Feasts are often celebrated in smaller circles, but we know that the real feast can only be celebrated with everyone together, with the whole of humanity, in fact, with the whole of creation. In a way, our celebration is part of a larger universal celebration, where there is food, animals, flowers and plants, water and wine, the sun and the sky, the moon and the evening breeze, perfumes and lights, colors and music, young and old, black and white, love and sympathy, speaking and listening, healing and touching, teaching and learning, singing and dancing, hugging and kissing, tears of joy and laughter, reconciliation and peacemaking, forgiveness for the past, and openness to the future, a future that cannot be but brilliant. It is an efficient, practical, and concrete *mystical* moment.

At the same time it is an aesthetic moment. It is the organization of our true potential in such an artful way that it reveals the full meaning of our lives. Isn't that what all art, literature, music, poetry, sculpture, architecture, painting, and drama is about? We know that the final outcome of our lives will be a great celebration, a feast. That is what the book of Revelation tells us:

> Then I saw a new heaven and a new earth, the first heaven and the first earth had disappeared now, and there was no longer any sea. I saw the Holy City, the new Jerusalem, coming down from God, out of heaven, as beautiful as a bride all dressed for her husband. Then I heard a loud voice call from the throne, "You see this city? Here God lives among men. He will make his home among them; they shall be his people, and he will be their God, his name is God-with-them. He will wipe away all tears from their eyes, there will be no more death, and no more mourning or sadness. The world of the past has gone.[3]

And the feast will start.

Lord of the Dance

Jesus constantly used the image of a feast or banquet to tell us what our lives are about, and he celebrated several feasts during his lifetime. It was, as we noticed in another chapter, the setting for the first of his "signs," a wedding at Cana. According to the author of Revelation, our final activity will be a wedding feast.

When Jesus met the apostles for the last time before his arrest and death, he celebrated the Passover with them. It was a feast that contained all the elements we have discussed: the company, the food, the drink, the interpretation, the past, the present, the future.

It was the celebration of the exodus from Egypt, in view of all the blessings still to come. In Jesus' time, the celebration of that liberation must also have reminded them of the slavery they lived in under Roman occupation. He invited them to commemorate him every time they would break their bread, every time they share wine in that festive way. Jesus described our actual situation as that of girls dressed up as bridesmaids waiting to be let in to the celebration. He also described our terrible fate in case we were not ready, when we would come too late or not be properly dressed. He insisted that God is preparing a banquet for all of us. He does not restrict the number of guests; all are invited. All the peoples of the world are to come with their treasure and their gifts to the final feast.

As we sing in *Jesus Is the Lord of the Dance,* "I have played the flute for you, and you did not dance!"[4] It was one of his most bitter complaints. The dance and the feast was to Jesus the real way to celebrate life. If we forget this, we make him unintelligible to people who hear about him for the very first time.

In 1846, the first Protestant, Lutheran, missionaries arrived in Mombasa, on the east coast of Africa. They built a small church and learned the language. One Sunday they opened their church and invited the local people. Fifteen came, all men, no women or children. The local population obviously did not trust the newcomers. The service is described in the diary of one of the missionaries. It was a Lutheran service: singing, but the singing of hymns without too much rhythm, preaching, long prayers, blessings, and, that first time, no communion.

When the service was over, the two German pastors, Krapf and Rebmann, asked their visitors for their impressions. The Warabai were quite ready to give them. They did not think too much of the services and they did not intend to come back. When asked why not, their answer was, "We do not worship like that!" Asked how they did worship, they said: "When we worship we celebrate a feast; there should be plenty of food, an oxen should be butchered, and there should be rice and fruits, singing and dancing."

The pastors responded by saying that the services were the way they were because they were sinners. The Warabai asked for an explanation of that term, and when it was given, they said: "Who told you those stories about us?"

When the missionaries said that God had not given up on them, and that he had sent his son Jesus to show his love and to save them, the Warabai answered that they did not need the story about Jesus to know that God loved them. Did God not give give them life, the sun and the moon, the drink and the food, the clothing, the salt, the meat, and all they needed?

Celebrating God could only be done in a real feast. Jesus would not have agreed more.

Alleluia, Praise the Lord

The Warabai organized their worship in such a way that they experienced a kind of mystical moment during it. During their celebrations they danced, drank, and ate in the kind of unity we described above. During those moments they realized what it means to be a human being, connected in the present with the past and opening up to a new future, together with all that they related to: animals, plants, fruits and all the other elements they were intimately living with. They had their doubts about the type of celebration those Western messengers of the "good news" brought. The *goodness* of that message must have been the reason for their doubt. I wonder if the same is not true for men and women today.

There are many contemporary characteristics that seem to make the celebration of a feast very difficult for us. We live so much in the passing moment that the commemoration of facts out of the past is difficult. We live on the sharp edge of the present. That lack of a sense of history causes us to forget the great deeds of God in the past. It makes us oblivious of the liberations we and our ancestors have experienced.

We are not only disconnected from the past, but also from one another and from nature around us. We hardly ever eat together. According to a research done by J. Angeline some years ago, the average North American family eats only three meals a week together. That number most likely has gone down still further. Since then, the introduction of gadgets such as the microwave oven has made our eating and drinking alone still easier.

In general, many church services are far from a celebration, even if the leader of the service might announce every Sunday that we are "celebrating" the mysteries of Jesus Christ, so that we might interpret and understand what is happening to us.

There is another difficulty that is felt more and more. Our

celebrations are practically always limited to our own group. We celebrate as Catholics, or Baptists, as Bahai or Muslims, as Mennonites or Jews. We cut ourselves off in that way from a real celebration. We aren't faithful to the diversities and varieties of human life we represent. We aren't faithful to ourselves or to the universe we are the center of. Justice has not yet been established among us. We still have much to learn. We still have a long way to go.

Yet, sometimes our celebrations do succeed, and the streets fill up, and the singing starts, and the dance spreads through the crowds. We still have some celebrations that bring us together. But there are so many exceptions. Perhaps it's because we know better than ever before that the real celebration can only be a global one. It will be all-inclusive or none at all. We must be confident that it will be all and everyone. That is how we were made, how we are, and how we will be.

One day humanity will arise in full splendor, clothed by the whole of nature. The visionaries who see us like that are becoming more numerous. Jesus definitely saw us in that way, together with himself. That is what he celebrated when he took the bread and broke it, when he took the wine and shared it: "This is my body; this is my blood." This meant at the same time: "This is our body; this is our blood!"

Alleluiah. Praise the Lord![5]

10

OUR

IMITATION OF JESUS

There is a story about a man who had joined Francis of Assisi because he esteemed Francis a saint. He wanted to be a saint, too, for several reasons. He thought that Francis would go to heaven, and he wanted to go to heaven, too. He saw how popular Francis was and always surrounded by all kinds of people, and he wanted that kind of popularity, too.

He did not know what to do about all this, wondered how he might become like Francis. One day he got a brilliant idea, at least, he thought it was brilliant. He reasoned, if I do exactly what Francis does, I have to be like him.

So he started to follow Francis everywhere. When Francis went into the forest, this brother would follow some steps behind him. When he saw Francis kneel down behind a bush, he would kneel down behind a bush. When he saw Francis stretching out his arms in prayer, he would stretch out his arms in prayer. When Francis would stop and go home, he would stop and go home.

One day Francis told the man to be himself. To follow someone in that way is childish and unhealthy. It means living totally outside of ourselves. Nothing genuine would come from within ourselves except that strange determination to be like someone else. It also means that all Christians with the same ideal would all be the very same, which is clearly an undesirable situation. We would not come a step further in our human history. We would not get a minute nearer to the maturing of the Kingdom of God among us. It would also be impossible, since we all live in different circumstances, in different places, at different times, with different genes, in a different culture. We all approach life from different angles. We all have different histories, and even though we might have lived at the same time, we have different sources and reserves of vitality, with peculiarities not shared with others.

For that reason it is impossible to give detailed guidelines or prescriptions for imitating someone. Each one of us sees the world in a different way, from a different point of view. It is like the diamond we spoke of earlier. One sees the diamond reddish, but someone else from another angle sees it as blue, or yellow, or orange.

Thus, we cannot even imitate Jesus in this way. It is impossible from all points of view, if we take that imitation as something totally literal. He lived in an other time, in another environment, in the midst of people with a mind-set different from ours, at another stage of human history, at a different point in human progress, or upward moving spiral.

To imitate him in this superficial way would mean that we would live completely from outside ourselves. Our direction signals would not come from within, but from without. Anything that comes only from without is no good. In fact, it would be evil for ourselves and for the community in which we live. The possibilities of that community, even its growth potential, are based on our personal differences. That variety, that richness underlies the biological richness of "personality."

> Each one of us, therefore, is the only person who can ultimately discover for him the attitude and the approach (which nobody else can imitate) that will make him cohere to the utmost possible degree with the surrounding universe as it continues its progres; that cohesion being, in fact, the state of peace which brings happiness.[1]

Impossible and Possible Imitation

Jesus said that his disciples should "follow" him. He never said, "Mimic me." Paul followed him later on, and so did Peter. He asked them to follow him, to walk after him. He asked them to be his disciples, to learn from him. The main lessons he gave in word and deed were the ones that prepared them for Pentecost, when they suddenly realized that they were with Spirit, the same Spirit that had made them call him Christ. He asked them to follow him on his inner journey, where he had discovered his own riches, being the child of God, full of divinity, full of potentiality. He invited them to make that journey to their inner self, to discover that same Spirit within themselves.

To "imitate" Jesus means to make that journey and to live by that Spirit from within. The living by that Spirit from within made them other Christs. They could not be other Jesuses. Jesus was unique, conceived in the womb of a mother they were not conceived in, born of a father they were not born of, in a town they were not born in. He had been in danger in a way they were never in. They never had to go to Egypt as refugees, as he and his family did. They did not have his experiences in Nazareth and the other places he was during the thirty years we don't know much about. He had a spiritual baptism from the hands of John none of them had undergone in the same way. He had been in the desert for forty days before they even met him. He had gone through temptations in a way they had not. He related to God in another way than they did, though he told them how he related to *Abba*. He was different, and he would remain different.

One thing they had in common: they lived from within; they lived from within the same Spirit in them. Jesus made it clear that they were like he was, that we are like he is, the same type of person, though with a different personality, a different history, and a different era. He made them understand how the Spirit wanted to insert them into a process that was going on in this world where something was happening: the giving birth to a new humanity. This was a process they would not see the end of while in this world, but some of his followers would see the end, as he himself foretold.

Being Engaged

Being taken up in a process means accepting the fact that we are not yet complete, that much has to happen within us and around us. It means that we can't answer yet the question: "Who are you?" We really don't know who we are. We are, and we are not yet; we are growing all the time. We are incomplete as persons and as a human society. We are being born, we are being hatched, but we are not yet there.

Jesus even refuses to answer the question "Who are you?" in a direct way. He turns the question around, asking the questioner, "Will you follow me?" Jurgen Moltmann puts this well when he says:

> Man is not thereby told who he is, in fact, basically, what he can and cannot do, what he should and should not do. A history is opened up to him into which God's promise will lead him in the future. A new possibility of beginning is opened up to him as a prospect, a possibility of being in community with God.[2]

Jesus was in the same and yet in a different position than we are. To know him, to know ourselves, we have to make the journey he made, a journey within, discovering who we are, in what universe we live. This is followed by a journey from within into that universe around us, making our lives part of a history we are an integral part of. Following Jesus means being engaged in his venture, a venture that is ours as well as his, because it is the venture of humanity being born.

Listlessness

Visiting a Sunday morning liturgy in an average Western church does not give the visitor the impression that the worshippers are involved in a dramatic struggle, the birth of a new humanity. There is much good will. The participation in the collections and the gathering of foodstuffs for the poor are signs of this, but there is scarcely a word on a rallying cry regarding the Kingdom of God on the scale Jesus dreamed about. Religion is something we seem to "possess." It is that idea of possession that makes us so certain that we are where we should be, and to stay where we are. In a sense, you might say, the Sunday congregation knows all about God; they don't have to search for God further. They have God in their church, so to speak, if not in their pocket.

Such an attitude closes many people off from anything around them. Why should they be interested in other views on God and society? Was Jesus not the answer to all their questions? In other words, Jesus is used to fix them in this present age forever. They are, in fact, no longer followers. They don't seem to be on a journey any more, certainly not the kind Jesus took. They are waiting for their death in order to be fixed as they are, eternally. Their ambitions are not Kingdom ambitious. They are trying to be as comfortable as possible and to make as much money as possible. They have lost all sense of mission and purpose. They have no inkling that they are supposed to be taken up in a process, developing, journeying. They are only waiting for an end, not the end of something that is really moving on. No, they are waiting for an end of their waiting for that end. No wonder we give the impression so often of utter boredom. No wonder the younger members of the congregation do not come to our liturgical celebrations, or, if they come, are yawning in the face of the gestures and words that should inspire, stimulate, and empower them.

The Needed Vision

All kinds of people interested in the famine and refugee problem in Africa had come together in Washington D.C. to discuss policies. They had been together before to discuss and study the causes of the problems in Africa. A booklet on the subject[3] sold out in no time. The research had been an eye-opener to many. The questions they were facing was what to do, what kind of development plan to use? They needed a plan to assist people in this country to help people in Africa to help themselves. "Don't just catch a fish for them; teach them how to fish." After a long discussion it was agreed that the relevant cultural, political, and economic viewpoints have deep spiritual roots, both in North America and Africa.

Poverty is an economic problem, or the result of unsolved economic problems. In a situation where some people are very rich while at the same time others are hungry, something has gone wrong in the systems of distribution of the goods given to all of us. Something has gone wrong with the original creation plan. The hunger problem has not only an ethical dimension, but next to the cultural, economic, and political aspects of it, even a spiritual dimension. There is not only something wrong with our structures, there is also something wrong with us. These problems lie as much within ourselves as within the realm of political or economic theory.

> Our inability to solve problems of economic theory lies partly in the lack of theoretical answers, but equally within the human failure to sufficiently "desire" and so re-order their economic priorities. This lack of "desire"—which, by the way, is not unconnected from "desire" for God— derives from an inability in the West to accept our inner poverty and incompleteness. We "desire" to fill our lives continuously. Such an attitude requires that poverty exists as somebody's else's problem rather than my own. Similarly, in the field of racism, Jung, and following him, Laurens van der Post, came to the conclusion that racism was finally attributable to our own inability to accept and face the shadow side, the dark, the unlit sides of our personality.

> Social and economic problems need, for their final solution, a rich attention to man's own inner dynamics, and only religion, or spirituality, properly understood, can enable this.[4]

We will never be able to do anything about ourselves, others, or the world as long as we have no vision or model of what we should be together. The older spiritual visions which were once very useful have fallen into disuse. They were once the high point we had reached in the spiral. They are now too individualistic, too tribalistic, too elite, too divisive, too otherworldly, too limited, too unrealistic, and now out of date. These visions do not come from within, from the way we follow Jesus, from our imitation of him. Sticking to them now would mean betraying ourselves and being unfaithful to our own journey.

The Needed Enthusiasm

We need more than a vision; we need the motivation to realize it. In a speech given some days after Christmas in Peking in 1943, Pierre Teilhard de Chardin divided humanity in three categories. He explained that there are three attitudes to life: those who are tired (or pessimists), those who are seeking pleasure (or hedonists), those who believe in the future (or enthusiasts).[5] The *tired ones* are those for whom existence is a failure, a mistake, fate, or bad luck. According to them, it would be better not to exist at all. This attitude is sometimes organized in a belief system like those in certain Asian spiritualities. It can be highly sophisticated, as some Western philosophies, but it can also reveal very common attitudes, such as: "What's the use of trying to find an answer? Why not leave the primitive people alone, leave the ignorant ignorant? What's the point of progress? Why write books? Why think? Why all that talking? Didn't you learn anything? It is always the same: There's nothing new under the sun!" When they sit in front of their television, the pessimists will only look at the programs that confirm them in their pessimism about humanity. In fact, all the programs they see seem to give them that very same message. "Let our hearts harden. Let our skin thicken. Let us cut off our contacts and restrict our needs. Let us sit in a corner, withdraw in our shell, and be at peace! Leave us alone, please!"

The *pleasure seekers* agree that it is better to be than not to be. For them, however, to be is to take your fill at the present moment. They are always busy trying to enjoy the present moment as much as possible. They are fun seekers all through. The weekend is not yet over and they are already looking for the adventure they'll have next weekend. Money becomes very important to enjoy life in this way. Money is the most important thing in life. That is not exactly true, because they use the money for their enjoyment.

But sometimes the possibility of enjoyment, created by the possession of money, makes money itself a source of contentment. You will hear people say: "Just imagine what I would be able to do if I had the money." This does not mean that they are going to do the kinds of things they intended to with the money. Having the money sometimes seems sufficient.

When they have had enough pleasure, they lie on the grass or the beach, with a flower in their mouth, looking up at the blue sky. Tomorrow will be another day to enjoy. They do not look any further. No wild dreams about the future, and no memories of the past either. They just live for the moment. They drink from life as much as they can, not to quench their thirst, or to restore their vigor, but simply from a desire to drain each new source. They turn life's moments around and around as one would turn a gem, catching a new color, a new shade, at every turn.

Let us seize the day. *Carpe diem!* Let us use all opportunities to enjoy life as much as possible. Consume! Let us take the easiest possible way of making money as fast as we can. Forget about others. Why should we think of them? Didn't they have the same opportunities we had? Let us drop everything that does not pay, even if it's useful for others. Forget about them. Explore and change constantly so that you may feel more fully, enjoy more deeply, be thrilled in a new way. The hedonists, which is what they really are, are always watching for new colors, new fashions, new shapes, new smells, new tastes, new restaurants, new countries, new sceneries, new love affairs. All the advertisments in our media seem made for them. Since producers of commercials have a keen sense of the market, pleasure seekers must form a great part, if not almost the whole, of that market. When they look at television, it is for new thrills, new sensations, even in the images of the misery of others, the hunger in Ethiopia or Chad. It all fits their idea of "entertainment." Even the giving they might do afterward is done because of the pleasure it gives them. Let us make the best of the moment we hold in our hands. Anyone who threatens our enjoyment of life is our enemy.

The *enthusiasts* sincerely think there is something important going on in this world. They believe in the possibility of a new and better world, a better humanity. They believe in growth, ascent, discovery, conscientization, and true human progress. For them, humanity is on a journey, but has not yet reached its goal. Full life is in front of us, still to be reached. That future fullness of life is a focal point of warmth and light we are slowly drawing closer to. The enthusiasts are full of hope not only for themselves, but for the whole of humanity.

Teilhard notes that we might sometimes laugh at such enthusiastic persons, and say that their vision is imagined. "But at the same time, it is they who have made us who we are, and it is from them that tomorrow's earth will emerge." We might discuss at length the value of these different points of view. We might think they manifest only a matter of taste or disposition, of character or education, but there is more to them than that. Nobody, whichever of the three categories he or she belongs to, could deny that something is happening around us and within us. That there is a movement and there is growth that seems to take place at each turn of the spiral. The growth that has taken place during our lifetime was described in Chapter 3, but growth on another level takes place again and again in human history.

If that is true, only the road that leads us in that direction will bring us happiness. It is the road walked, and sometimes run, by the enthusiasts. It leads to greater self-insight, to greater interest in others, to a greater, wider, more conscious, more intelligent, and more spiritual human community.

It is not difficult to make out to what category Jesus of Nazareth belongs.

Jesus: Enthusiastic Visionary, Visionary Enthusiast

In all the descriptions of Jesus, we get the impression of a highly versatile and enthusiastic person. After an apparently very long period of maturing he suddenly burst onto the local scene, and in fact onto the world scene, when he realizes that the Spirit of God was with him after his baptism by John.

Although very open to the enjoyments of life—he is even accused of being too good an eater and drinker—and surrounded by people and a world he loved, he looked through the situation as it presented itself, and he saw something different: another world, another humanity, another relationship to the Transcendent One. He not only saw this, he worked toward it. He broke through the restrictions of his family and people, their taboos and laws.

He kept to those relationships and laws, but he went further. He contacted others, being as universal as he could be, considering the means of transportation and communication at his disposal. He was so enthusiastic and he believed so strongly in his dream that he did not hesitate to die for it, foretelling that he and his ideal would remain with us forever. His dream came, he said, from *Abba*. He left his followers a task, a journey to take, a road to travel. We have to take that road if we want to follow him.

There are three journeys, and they all have to be made if we want to be like other Christs, other anointed ones.

Journey 1: The Inward Journey

A Jewish scholar from New York invited me one day to visit him in a hotel, in Nairobi, Kenya, where I was at the time. I was very surprised by the invitation, which is one of the reasons I went to see him. He told me that he read my book, *"Jesus the Stranger."*[6] He said Jesus was always a mystery to him, and he told me why: "We don't know his teachers. At the feet of what teacher had he sat?" He added that he did not have that problem with Paul. We know that he was Gamaliel's disciple, and that is why we can place him. But who taught Jesus? Where did he get his insights?

He said that one day we will know. We will find one or another document somewhere in a cave or basement with the information about Jesus' early years, just as we found the Gnostic writings and the Qumran documents that taught us so much about Christianity and Judaism around the time of Jesus. Until we find that information, which according to my host must have been hidden or destroyed on purpose, we can only guess at Jesus' teachers.

Many have guessed. Some say Jesus spent his "hidden" years in the Far East. Who can tell? One thing, however, is transparent: Whatever happened to him, whether he stayed in Nazareth, somewhere else in Palestine, or even in a far away place, he had made a very thorough inner journey before he started to make his public appearances.

He had become very conscious of himself and had reached a high degree of inner unification and personalization. He must have made a very intense journey inward, when we first hear about him. We see and hear him introduce more order and more unity in his ideas, his feelings, and his behavior. Before each decision he withdraws not so much into nature—the mountaintops, the wild, or the desert—but into himself. We are constantly told that he withdrew to solitary places.[7]

The best example is when Luke tells how the Holy Spirit came over him while he was praying after his baptism by John the Baptizer. Immediately after that he went into the desert to digest what had happened to him. It was another of his inward journeys, but now one that would bring him on another, an outward bound, track. If we follow Jesus, we will have to follow him on that inward route. We will have to work to achieve, from the spiritual, intellectual, artistic, and moral point of view, our own inner perfection, revealing in ourselves our own dimensions and possibilities. We will have to become aware of our strengths and weaknesses, our charisms and talents, in order to know what gift we are to ourselves and to the world around us. We have to find ourselves.

That will mean hard work, through and beyond matter. It will mean a participation in what is going on within and around us, taking note of what others discover in the many ways humanity expresses itself, especially within the cultural group we belong to. This belonging is a very important part of our make-up. Jesus, too, considered the cultural group he belonged to a very important part of his make-up. Yet, it is on this inward journey that we personalize ourselves; we free ourselves from the older bonds that once were necessary and useful but now no longer serve their purpose.

After Jesus had left them, his family (including his

mother) and townsfolk asked him to come back. They thought he had become mad and wanted to bring him to his senses. They wanted to bring him back into the circle from which he had liberated himself. He would later tell his apostles to leave persons and things behind for the sake of his Kingdom! Jesus revealed the results of this inward journey best with his farewell at the Last Supper, especially as told in that marvelous report of that occasion described in John's gospel. It is, in a way, his commentary on the Our Father he had taught them to pray. In those last words he revealed how he relates to *Abba* and how *Abba* relates to him, and to humanity; how because of this relationship he and all human beings belong together; how he, the Father, and the Spirit are in them; how love should be our life force as it was and is his; how all this had led him on that second journey, outward.

Journey 2: The Outward Journey

The danger of the journey inward is obvious. We have to react against the possibility of too much attention to our own personality; we close in on ourselves. That danger will not exist when our inward journey is authentic. Sometimes it isn't, as Teilhard puts it:

> An elementary temptation or illusion lies in wait for the reflective center which each one of us nurses deep inside him. It is present from the very birth of that center; and it consists in fancying that in order to grow greater each one of us should withdraw into the isolation of his own self, and egoistically pursue in himself alone the work, peculiar to him, of his own fulfillment, that we must cut ourselves off from others, or translate everything in terms of ourselves.[8]

Coming out of the desert, Jesus was immediately confronted with this very temptation. The "opponent" tempted him to use for himself alone the fruits of his inward journey and the divine powers he had discovered in himself. He refused and gradually started to open up more and more to others around him, making all kinds of contacts. His first healings are in an almost tribal and family context. The mother-in-law of Simon was healed because she was his mother-in-law. The people at Cana were his friends. He preached to his own people in Nazareth—without too much success.

But then he traveled more widely, contacting people of other convictions and representing other cultures: Samaritans, pagans, and Romans. In several cases he was amazed about their beliefs and visions, about their zeal and their piety.[9] He traveled over his region and settled in the most cosmopolitan town, Capernaum, a harbor town. He was especially interested in the groups that were neglected or oppressed. He broke through the barriers that isolated the sick and poor from him. He talked with women he was not supposed to talk to. He protected an adulterous woman. He allowed children in his presence, although his followers did not like the idea.

He not only related to fellow human beings around him— the old and the young, the abled and the disabled—he related to his whole environment. His words and deeds were full of reference to animals and plants, birds and fishes, sky and the sea. There were foxes, doves, camels, donkeys, snakes, sparrows, gnats, all kinds of fish, plants, seeds, weeds, grass, lilies, olive trees, vines, sun and moon, rocks, sand, lakes, coins, pearls, water, salt, yeast, light, fire, darkness, and finally bread and wine. He sinks his roots deep into the rich, tangible, material realities that surrounded him.[10]

All privileges fell away and were declared invalid. On his outward journey he championed "the other." He forbade the use of the name enemy. Enemies should be friends. We should not try to separate ourselves from one another, but should grow more united. In this way he inserted himself in the racial, tribal, and "apartheid" fights that rage among us. He favored reconciliation and forgiveness, breaking bread and forming one body. He condemned the rich, who were heartless, and he opted for the poor. He praised the poor widow in the temple—Did she remind him of his mother?— in front of the leaders, scribes, and the rich.

He constantly tried to affirm the oppressed by paying attention to their questions and answers, their insights and needs. He was a liberator who developed their sense of self-worth. On his outward journey he developed much of his salvation and liberation theology.

Journey 3: To the Center

Finally, Jesus announced to his followers that he was going to Jerusalem. They protested because they feared he was going to be murdered there. After all the personal contacts he had made, he went to the place some considered the center of the world, where in final instance, according to the prophecies, all people would come together for their final transfiguration, where God's banquet with his people would take place.

All his experiences came together in this Holy City. He was received by enthusiastic allies—the people, the animals, the palm branches, the people's garments, and even the stones that would shout in case the people were hindered from doing so. He entered the temple—it was one of the last days before Passover—and upset the tables of the money changers, and drove out the vendors. He made it impossible to carry on the temple service. Having done this, he finally comes to his point: "My house will be called a house of prayer for all the people!"[11] The time of discrimination and privileges are over.

The great rallying together of the whole of humanity has started. The messianic prophecies are going to be fulfilled. That same evening, according to Mark's gospel, the chief priests and scribes tried to find some way of doing away with him.

Some days later we find him with his disciples at what he knew would be their last supper. On that occasion, he took bread and broke it, saying, "This is my body!," and sharing the cup of wine, he said, "This is my blood!" They were to repeat these words after him, forming with him one body under the influence of the life-giving Spirit.

Brought together in that small circle, it was their affection for him and one another that kept them together. Their eating and drinking together made them one in a very special way, as he explained during the meal. Their togetherness would have to expand in circles of ever-increasing radius. It was the formation of the new cosmic egg that in final instance would bring all together under the organizing principle of the Spirit: new heart and new soul.

Would it work? Would this movement be blessed? Would the new change-over, the metanoia, which he introduced while celebrating the old Passover with them, work? Was it according the divine plan of development among us? Would it be acceptable to God? The apostles were hesitant. Without asking for it, they wanted to have a sign, an affirmation from above. After the meal he went with them to pray in the garden in the dark of night. What happened afterward must have been considered coincidence. To him, it was not. While at prayer, and while struggling on a new journey inward, he was arrested, bound up, and taken away. The rest of the story is so well known that we need not repeat it here.

An Asian Jew was condemned by a Roman from Europe, while a man from Africa helped him carry his cross. While hanging on the cross, his opponents asked him to show his power, that he was blessed by God. They taunted him to save himself, but he died. All seemed to be over. Most of his followers disappeared; even those who did not run away could think only of arranging his burial. It seemed that the new principle of life and organization he had introduced among us, and around that table, was nipped in the bud. No chance whatsoever. Heaven and earth remained closed. In fact, the whole of creation seemed to groan at the moment of his death. It had become dark in the middle of the day, and the animals and birds went into hiding. The sun had disappeared. The earth rumbled and shifted in something that seemed to be agony. Some dead came out of their graves and only added to the utter confusion. Judas was swinging from a tree. All life and promise of life seemed to have gone. A cock had crowed at the final betrayal. Instead of indicating a new beginning, that crow seemed to signify the end. The only positive note came from a foreigner, a soldier, who said, "He was a good man!"

All his journeys, the inner, the outer, and the centered, were over. The tomb in which he was buried, as in the shell of an enormous egg, seemed to contain only a dead germ. Until the third day, when the shell broke and he rose from death to show that he had come to introduce the promise of life and God's eternal blessing. Alleluia!

The circle around him formed again; first the women, then the men. He ate with them and told them how important it is to forgive anything that happened for the sake of the peace he brought.

Finally, having restored that small circle as a nucleus of an expansive movement that would reach to all and everything, he sent them out into the world. He did not leave them for good. He will come back, once all have been taken up in the movement he initiated. All those born from Adam, the man-woman born from Mother Earth and the Spirit of God, will be collected together again. At that moment all will be one again. Christ will be the name of this divine Earthchild, in whom all will find final fulfillment, and only in him.

Our Journeys

One day a postgraduate student handed me part of his work on the history of the church in Kenya. We had a discussion about traditional educational methods of the African society he belonged to. We discussed the value of storytelling in an educational process. We agreed that it was the only feasible way of communicating values. "But," he said, "you should not forget that we tell our stories differently than you do in the West." I was surprised and asked him what the difference was. He explained that in the African system a story is told without the moralizing lesson after the story. He added that the storyteller tries to render the story in such a way that the listeners can identify with the characters in the story, and that they are supposed to draw the lesson themselves. If you explain the story afterward and tell what the lesson of the story is, the instruction comes from outside the story, and it should come from within. It does come from within if you leave the conclusion to the listener.

This is also true of the story about Jesus. Having been told about his journeys and adventures, his dreams and ideals, it is up to everyone to draw the conclusion and to map her or his own ways. Let us give, however, some concluding hints.

First, we have to imitate Jesus on his journey inward. We will always need our moments of solitude, of turning inward, of being with ourselves and in the deepest depth of ourselves with the unspeakable presence of God we depend on. This presence knows our name, revealing it and yet always hiding it, as Etty Hillesum described so beautifully. This journey inward will bring us further, as it did Jesus.

Following him on his journey outward will mean an active interest in others, in their culture and religious heritage, in their social systems and their economic welfare. This contact can only enrich us. It will bring out potential in ourselves we never thought of. Following Jesus will mean involving ourselves in the world around us in such a way that oppression is overcome, that everyone is liberated, and that our environment is respected. It will mean the end of exploitation in any form. It will mean a change in the way we carry on business and engage in politics.

Imitation of Jesus demands the reorganization of our service and distribution systems, which only serve some, and therefore are in fact of no service at all. Wherever anyone suffers, we all suffer, as Jesus made very clear. In our compassion, we all know this. Our following of Jesus should open us to the need and misery of others, or, we should say, *to our need and to our misery.*

On our outward journey we developed much of our personalistic, liberational, and creational spirituality, as Jesus did. He sent us on the same journey, the same mission. We should walk the same path, following him. Now and then we should rest and celebrate. All should be invited to our celebration and all should participate.

Our celebration should offer the motivation needed to continue to progress, to love, and to forgive, to beget and educate children in Christ-like potential and attitudes that will grow from generation to generation the more we love one another.

Slowly the spiral along which we are moving upward and forward will form more and more a network around the center, from which all flows forth and to which all flows back. The center is the pulsing heart of love, God's. The beginning of this lofty vision is already here, a vague picture of a model human being and of an ultimate unified world society.

The Cosmic Egg and Our Mysticism

This brings us back to the beginning of this book, to the visions and feelings that point to the future.

The experience that we are one
with the whole of nature,
with the whole of humanity,
with the whole of creation.
The experience of a transcendency
that attracts us
every time we feel attracted by one of its creatures,
especially when that attraction is based
on our differences,
on being man or woman,
on being black or white,
on giving God this name or that,
on dancing one way or another,
on believing this or that,
on singing here or there.
The experience of not being ready,
of not being at the end of the journey,
of not having arrived,
of not knowing our own name,
of discovering again and again
unexpected vistas in our souls and our hearts,
hopes until then unknown,
loves until then not even guessed.
Being constantly in tension,
in conflict and contradiction,
in a dialectical struggle with others,
and with ourselves,
being afraid of being dissolved,
and knowing that we can't do it alone.

The feeling of being born,
and yet not born,
of belonging to one ethnic group,
and of belonging to all,
of singing and not knowing the final words,
of being named and yet being nameless,
of being in a shell
with all the others
as in an egg,
from which all together
we will break out
one day,
shouting "Alleluia,"
the hour has come,
the birth pangs are over.

EPILOGUE

Should we end here? Should we stop at that moment when all will be assembled together with Jesus the Christ, forming the one and glorious transfigured human being, with whom everyone will have a unique and total loving relationship with the whole of our human and earthly universe in all its variety and richness, in all its expressions and forms? We seem to be so accustomed to tasks and missions. We like our rest, our weekends, the moments when the stimulation is over and the joy breaks through. We also like our work, our activity, and the tensions it provokes and dissipates.

Besides, there are all those actual inspirations and intuitions. Not only are our science fiction books and cinemas filled with extra-terrestrial beings, even our scientists have put up their sensors and antennae to catch any possible sign of a presence out there. Are we the only intelligent beings in the universe? Are there any others in the enormous expanse around us?

There have always been rumors about extra-terrestrial creatures. Once they were called angels and archangels. There were different types of those creatures, cherubims and seraphims. Some of them even had personal names, such as Michael and Gabriel. "Angel" seems to have been used in another sense also. The Book of Revelation refers to the seven presiding spirits of Ephesus, Smyrna, Pergamum, Thyatira, Sardis, Philadelphia, and Laodicea. The text gives the impression that those Christian communities were considered to be angels when counted together as a community.

Would it be possible that Christ is the name of an angel, the name of humanity at the end of its development and spiritualization? Who will tell? Who knows? Here, we are in theo-fiction.

But would it not be possible, and even probable, that once we are out of the shell of our cosmic egg, in which we are still growing, we will face a whole new host of creatures as the next invitation to grow and grow? Did not some of us entertain angels already, as the author of the letter to the Hebrews suggested when he gave us the advice to welcome strangers?[1]

> The things
> that no eye has seen,
> and no ear has heard,
> things beyond the mind of man,
> all that God has prepared
> for those who love him.[2]

Even at the end we will only be at the start.

NOTES

Introduction

1. American author John Updike, to give only one example, wrote about Rev. George W. Hunt's study of his work: "In the course of looking through, over the years, his evolving commentary, I have been more than once startled, many times enlightened, and constantly grateful." *John Updike and the Three Great Secret Things: Sex, Religion and Art* (Grand Rapids, Mich.: Eerdmans, 1980).

2. In her book *The Aquarian Conspiracy* (Los Angeles: Tarcher, 1980), p. 367, Marilyn Ferguson remarks: "Needleman said Westerners were moving away from the form and trappings of Judaism and Christianity, 'not because they had stopped searching for transcendental answers to the fundamental questions of human life, but because that search has now intensified beyond measure.' "

3. Iris Murdoch, *The Philosopher's Pupil* (New York: Penguin Books, 1983), p. 571.

Chapter 1

1. Forest Reid, *Following Darkness* (London: Arnold, 1902), p. 42.

2. William James, *The Varieties of Religious Experience* rev. ed. (London: Longmans, Green and Co., 1902), p. 348.

3. John Updike, "The Artist and His Audience," *The New York Review of Books* (1985, XXXIII, no. 12), p. 14.

4. Quoted R.C. Zaehner, *Mysticism, Sacred and Profane* (New York: Oxford University Press, 1961), p.53.

5. Thomas à Kempis, *The Imitation of Christ,* translated by Leo Sherley-Price (London: Penguin Books, 1983), p. 50.

6. Luchesius Smits, *Omgaan met de Dood,* (Etten: Vormings Instituut, West Brabant, 1985), p. 28.

7. Yevgeny Yevtushenko, *Wild Berries* (New York: Morrow, 1984), p. 296.

8. Fred Alan Wolf, *Starwave Mind, Consciousness and Quantum Physics* (New York: Macmillan, 1984).

9. Mark 3:33-35.

10. London:, Gollancz, 1951, pp. 78-79.
11. *The Nag Hammadi Library* (San Francisco: Harper & Row, 1978), p. 126.

Chapter 2

1. Charles Y. Glock and Rodney Stark, *Religion and Society in Tension* (Chicago: Rand McNally, 1965), p. 158.
2. Kurt Back and Linda Brookover Bourque, "Can Feelings Be Enumerated?" *Behavioral Science* (Vol. 15, 1970, pp. 487-96.)
3. A.M. Greeley, *The Sociology of the Paranormal* (London: Sage Publications), 1975.
4. David Hay, *Exploring Inner Space* (New York: Penguin Books, 1982), pp. 118-19.
5. Hay, p. 125.
6. New York: Vintage Books, 1981, p. 144.
7. Hay, p. 137.
8. Matt. 16:16.
9. Matt. 16:17.
10. J. G. Donders, *Creation and Human Dynamism* (Mystic, Conn.: Twenty-Third Publications, 1985), p. 48. According to speech experts, the sounds *a* and *b* are respectively the first vowel and consonant a baby can pronounce in whatever language group a baby belongs to. The combination of the two sounds, abba or baba, are used by those babies for their mother and their father. So when Jesus told them to pray: "Our Abba, who art in heaven," no gender preference might have been meant.
11. John 10: 33-34.
12. 35.4-7 and 50.28-30, conflated, in *The Nag Hammadi Library*, ed. James M. Robinson (San Francisco: Harper & Row, 1981), pp. 119 and 129.
13. Hay, p. 133-34.
14. Simone Weil, *Waiting for God* (New York: Harper Colophon Books, 1973), p. 62.
15. Weil, p. 69.
16. *Ibid.*
17. *Hymn of the Universe* (New York: Harper Torch Books, 1983), p. 43.
18. Teilhard, pp. 47-48.
19. Teilhard, p. 53.
20. *Ibid.*

Chapter 3

1. A.H. Smits, *Bewustzijnsvernauwing en Bewustzijnsverruiming in de Theologie vanuit de Theorie van de Wereldconcepten* (Tilburg: Theologische Faculteit, 1985), p. 11.

2. *De Nieuwe Katechismus, Geloofsverkondiging voor Volwassenen,* in opdracht van de Bisschoppen van Nederland (Hilversum-Antwerpen: 's-Hertogenbosch, Roermond-Maaseik, 1966).
3. *A New Catechism* (New York: Herder and Herder, 1967).
4. Smits, p. 14,
5. Lima: CEP, 1971.
6. *A Theology of Liberation* (Maryknoll, N.Y.: Orbis Books, 1973).
7. Maryknoll, N.Y.: Orbis Books, 1970.
8. Paolo Freire, *Pedagogy of the Oppressed* (New York: Continuum, 1968).
9. For an excellent working out of this method in an African context, see Anne Hope and Sally Timmel, *Training for Transformation: A Handbook for Community Workers* (Gweru, Zimbabwe: Mambo Press, 1984).
10. See Edward L. Cleary, O.P., *Crisis and Change, The Church in Latin America Today* (Maryknoll, N.Y.: Orbis Books, 1984), pp. 74-79.
11. Hildegard of Bingen, quoted in *Illuminations of Hildegard of Bingen: Text by Hildegard of Bingen with Commentary by Matthew Fox* (Santa Fe, N.M.: Bear and Company, 1985), p. 36.

Chapter 4

1. Charles Singer and C. Rabin, *A Prelude to Modern Science, Being a Discussion of the History, Sources and Circumstances of the "Tabulae Anatomicae Sex" of Vesalius* (Cambridge, Eng.: Cambridge University Press, 1920).
2. *Revelationes Gertrudianae ac Mechtildianae, II Sanctae Mechtildis virginis ordinis sancti Benedicti Liber Specialis Gratiae,* ed. Solesmensium O.S.B. Monachorum (Paris, 1877), p. 18. *(De quattor pulsibus cordis Christi).*
3. See *Omgaan met de Dood.* In the interpretation of the data I differ with Smits.

Chapter 5

1. Joseph Epes Brown, *The Spiritual Legacy of the American Indian,* 4th printing (Wallingford, Penn.: Pendle Hill Pamphlet 135, 1964).
2. *Ibid.* p. 25.
3. *Ibid.* p. 26.
4. *Iedereen weet het beter* (The Hague: Querido, 1955).
5. Joseph Campbell, *Primitive Mythology,* rev. (London: Penguin Books, 1969), *passim.*
6. Matt. 23: 37.
7. John 16: 7.
8. Matt. 13: 52.
9. Rev. 21:26. For a remarkable description this "movement" brought by Jesus in this world see Walter Buehlmann's *"The Chosen Peoples* (Slough, England: St. Paul's Publications, 1982).
10. 1 Cor. 5:28.

11. See Chapter 8, "Healing Ourselves."
12. *Religion in America*, (Gallup Report No. 222). The Princeton Religion Research Center (March 1984), p. 56.
13. *Presentation on Culture*, CMSM Documentation, 40, (November 23, 1984), p. 10.
14. *Ibid*, p. 10.
15. John 16:20-23.
16. Rom. 8: 18-24.
17. See J. E. Cirlot, *A Dictionary of Symbols*, second edition (New York: Philosophical Library, 1971), p. 94.
18. *Ibid*.
19. See Matthew Fox, *Illuminations of Hildegard von Bingen*, p. 35.
20. *Ibid*. p. 36.

Chapter 6

1. 1 Sam. 3: 1-11.
2. Etty van Hillesum, *Het verstoorde leven, Dagboek van Etty van Hillesum, 1941-1943*, 5th printing (Haarlem: De Haan, 1981). English translation: *An Interrupted Life: The Diaries of Etty van Hillesum 1941-1943* (New York: Washington Square Press, 1985).
3. *Ibid*. p. 219.
4. *Ibid*. p. 81.
5. *Ibid*. p. 214.
6. *Ibid*. p. 217-18.
7. *Ibid*. p. 215.
8. *Ibid*. p. 160.
9. *Ibid*. p. 239.
10. *Ibid*. p. 218.
11. *Ibid*. p. 207.
12. *Ibid*. p. 161.
13. Quoted in Smits, *Omgaan met de Dood* o.c. p. 32-33, from C.L. Schulzberger, *De groten der aarde over dood en paradijs* (Amsterdam: De Tijd, 26 Augustus 1983), p. 43.
14. Gal. 4: 6-7.
15. Edward Schillebeeckx, *Het Kerkelijk Ambt, Voorgangers in de Gemeente van Jezus Christus* (Bloemendaal: H. Nelissen, 1980).
16. Robert N. Bellah, ed., *Habits of the Heart: Individualism and Commitment in American Life* (Berkeley: University of California Press, 1985), p. 233.
17. See Evelyn Underhill, *Mysticism: A Study in the Nature and Development of Man's Spiritual Consciousness*, Part Two (New York: A.P. Dutton, 1981), pp. 167-453.
18. Bellah, p. 248.
19. *Ibid*. p. 248 quoting from Parker J. Palmer, *Company of Strangers: Christians and the Renewal of America's Public Life* (New York: Crossroad, 1981), p. 155.

20. See Gustavo Gutierrez, *We Drink From Our Own Wells* (Maryknoll, N.Y.: Orbis Books, 1984), p. 16.

21. See Donal Dor, *Spirituality and Justice* (Maryknoll, N.Y.: Orbis Books, 1984), p. 16.

22. See J. Severino Croatto, *Exodus, a Hermeneutics of Freedom* (Maryknoll, N.Y.: Orbis Books, 1981).

23. See Matthew Fox, *Original Blessing: A Primer in Creation Spirituality* (Santa Fe, N.M.: Bear & Company, 1983).

24. Brian Swimme, *The Universe Is a Green Dragon: A Cosmic Creation Story"* (Santa Fe, N.M.: Bear & Company, 1985), p. 162.

25. *Ibid.* p. 170
26. John 3:11.
27. Mark 9:49.
28. Luke 12:49.
29. Acts 2:3.
30. Matt. 3:16.
31. Luke 3:21-22.
32. Luke 4:17-18.

Chapter 7

1. John 3:4.
2. Acts 2:35.
3. Acts 2:44-46.
4. Acts 4:32 and 33-34.
5. Acts 5:9.
6. Acts 6:1.
7. Matt. 25:37-40.
8. John 7:37-38.
9. John 7:39.
10. John 6:63.
11. Lewis Thomas, *The Lives of a Cell* (New York: Bantam Books, 1984).

Chapter 8

1. New York: Harper & Row, 1984.
2. *Ibid.* p. 5.
3. *Ibid.* p. 12.
4. *Ibid.* p. 6.
5. *Ibid.* pp. 44-45.
6. John 2:4-5.
7. Matt. 22:2; 4; 9. 25, 10; see also Rev. 19:7-9.
8. Teilhard, *ibid.* p. 45.
9. John 14:12.
10. Matt. 10:39.
11. 1 Thes. 4:17.

12. Eph. 4:16.
13. Eph. 4:24.
14. Eph. 4:26.
15. Eph. 3:6.
16. For further information, see Peter Lemesurier, *Beyond All Belief* (Tisbury, England: Element Books, 1983); Peter Russel, *The Awakening Earth* (London: Routledge and Kegan Paul, 1982); Fritjof Capra, *The Turning Point* (New York: Simon and Schuster, 1982); and the publications of World Future Society, Bethesda, Maryland.
17. See definition in *The American Heritage Dictionary*, 2nd ed. (Boston: Houghton and Mifflin Company, 1982): "serendipity n. The faculty of making fortunate and unexpected discoveries by accident [From its possession by the characters in the Persian fairy tale *The three princes of Serendip]*."
18. 12th ed. (New York: Simon and Schuster, 1979), p. 257.
19. Rom. 8:28.
20. See Chapter 2.

Chapter 9

1. This chapter uses, in its analysis and description of a festive celebration, data collected during research done in 1970-1971 with the students of Saint Thomas Aquinas Regional Seminary in Langata, Nairobi, and of the Department of Philosophy and Religious Studies at the University of Nairobi in Kenya. Nowhere does one know a feast as in Africa.
2. *African Philosophy and Religions* (Nairobi: Heinemann, 1969).
3. Rev. 21: 1-5.
4. See Matt. 11:17; Luke 7:13.
5. For a beautiful description of this celebration aspect of reality, of our cosmic unity, and the justice involved, see the texts already mentioned in Hildegard von Bingen's *Illuminations*, especially visions 15-25.

Chapter 10

1. Pierre Teilhard de Chardin, *On Love and Happiness* (San Francisco: Harper & Row, 1984), p. 76.
2. *Man* (London: SPCK, 1983), p. 17, quoted in Melvyn Matthews, "Religion as Disguise, *Areopagus* (Issue No. 12, October 1983) Bristol University, p. 1.
3. Bill Rau, *Feast to Famine* (Africa Faith and Justice Network, Box 29378, Washington DC 20017, 1985), p. 62.
4. Matthews, *ibid.* p. 2.
5. See "The Theoretical Axes of Happiness" in *On Love and Happiness*, pp. 56-82.
6. Maryknoll N.Y.: Orbis Books, 1978.